Cape Breto

A Park Lover's Companion

Masked Shrew

Dedicated to
Lucy, Danny, Stuart and Audrey

Cape Breton HIGHLANDS National Park

~ A Park Lover's Companion ~

Clarence Barrett

Breton Books
Wreck Cove

Book Editor & Designer: Ronald Caplan
Production Assistant: Bonnie Thompson

For help with this project, the author wishes to thank Pixie Williams and Dave McCorquodale; and, for the maps in Chapter 5, Dawn Allen. Geological diagrams in Chapter 3 are modelled after Goldthwaite, Johnson, and Rowland.

COVER PHOTOGRAPHS: Thanks to Warren Gordon, Gordon Photographic, for Keltic Lodge on Middle Head, with part of Highlands Links Golf Course. All other photographs are by Clarence Barrett. FRONT COVER: Looking south from French Mountain, Chéticamp Island in background; and the ocean at Black Brook. BACK COVER: Chéticamp River canyon; autumn sugar maples near the Lone Shieling; backcountry camping near Lone Lake, eastern highlands.

Publisher's Note
The Park is always changing. Check current trail maps and information at the Visitor Information Centres, and with the wardens.

How to Convert Measurements
Metric to imperial: 1 centimetre (cm) = 0.4 inch (in)
1 metre (m) = 1.1 yard (yd) or 3.3 feet (ft)
1 kilometre (km) = 0.6 mile (mi)
Imperial to metric: 1 inch (in) = 2.5 centimetres (cm)
1 yard (yd) = 0.9 metre (m)
1 mile (mi) = 1.6 kilometres (km)

We gratefully acknowledge generous support for this project from Fortress of Louisbourg Volunteers Association.

We acknowledge the support of
the Canada Council for the Arts for our publishing program.

 Canada Council **Conseil des Arts**
for the Arts **du Canada**

We also acknowledge support from
Cultural Affairs, Nova Scotia
Department of Tourism and Culture.

NOVA SCOTIA
Tourism and Culture

National Library of Canada Cataloguing in Publication
Barrett, Clarence, 1947-
    Cape Breton Highlands National Park : a park lover's companion / Clarence Barrett. — 1st ed.
ISBN 1-895415-62-4
    1. Cape Breton Highlands National Park (N.S.)—Guidebooks.
2. Trails—Nova Scotia—Cape Breton Highlands National Park—Guidebooks.   3. Hiking—Nova Scotia—Cape Breton Highlands National Park—Guidebooks.   I. Title.
FC2314.C36B37 2002   917.16'91   C2002-902890-6
F1039.C19B37 2002

CONTENTS

CONTINUED...

Prologue

ON A SUMMER EVENING, high on the tableland of Cape Breton Highlands, I'm rolling along on a bicycle through a landscape that's bathed in the golden light of a declining sun. From out of steep-sided valleys come the flute-like notes of hermit thrushes. There is no traffic and the air carries a faint perfume of balsam. Apart from the ethereal song of the birds, the mountains are shrouded in silence.

At the top of a long grade I dismount and look back across the broad rolling plateau. My gaze wanders over a patchwork of wild woods and open moorland. Crowds of ragged spruce and fir, their wind-beaten branches punctuated by the gray spikes of weathered snags, are interspersed with scattered openings of heath plants and feathery tamaracks. The scene is compelling.

Years before, I had stopped my bicycle here on an evening like this and listened to the same haunting call. I was fifteen, on my first trip through Cape Breton Highlands National Park. As a teenager, I had made frequent bicycle trips around the island's northern peninsula, either alone or with a school buddy who was always up for an adventure. It was on one of those trips, on an evening similar to this, that I remember looking across these same scraggy barrens and wondering what was "out there" beyond the guardrail, and where we would end up if we just started walking. The scene reminded me of Kipling's verse:

> Something hidden, Go and find it,
> Go and look behind the ranges—
> Something lost behind the Ranges,
> Lost and waiting for you. Go!

With a wildheartedness that was fostered by a diet of adventure comics, Robert Louis Stevenson and the tales of Scott and Shackleton, we talked of what it might be like to strike off across the plateau, and to emerge weeks later, tanned and grizzled, on the other side. About that time I came across a map of Cape Breton Highlands National Park that had names like "The Everlasting Barrens" and "Caribou Barrens" printed across broad areas of untracked terrain. There was something magnetic about those blank spaces on the map. The map had illustrations of bears and lynx, and near the centre of the Park it showed a small triangle with the words "White Hill, 1747 ft., highest point in Nova Scotia." The map also showed the Chéticamp River starting in a lake on the eastern side of the Park and flowing westward to the sea. I thought if I could get to its headwaters I might be able to float down the river in a rubber dinghy. I also found a report by Hugh Fletcher of the Geological Survey of Canada in which he gave a description of this northern part of Cape Breton. In 1886 Fletcher had written, "The Chéticamp River, for 10 or 12 miles of its length and in several of its tributaries, flows in gloomy, dangerous and all but impassible defiles, shut in by high mural cliffs."

That clinched it. I thought if Alexander MacKenzie could journey across Canada to the Pacific Ocean, surely I could find a way across the top of Cape Breton from the Atlantic to the Gulf of St. Lawrence. I'd heard something about a trail, an old fire road, that crossed the Park from somewhere around Mount Franey in Ingonish and went close to Chéticamp Lake. Maybe we could find it.

One summer, during school holidays, a friend—Alexander MacLeod—and I set out from Ingonish with a rubber boat and rucksacks full of canned goods, enough to do us for several days. We didn't know where the trail began and we didn't care. With the aid of a primitive compass and a small-scale map that was hardly better than a highway map, we started bushwacking in the general direction of Chéticamp Lake. After several hours of clawing our way through windfalls, bogs and spruce thickets, we caught a glimpse of the Mount Franey fire tower not very far behind us, and realized that at the rate we were going Chéticamp Lake would probably be frozen over by the time we got to it. We also realized that we were woefully under-equipped in terms of food, gear and experience. Especially experience. As adventurous and full of the vigour of youth as we were, we had enough common sense to turn back.

That first hike in Cape Breton Highlands National Park was not a rousing success. But from it I realized what wonderful opportunities there were in the Park for exploring—if we could just match our skills with our enthusiasm. And it was enough to make me want to return. Some of those first misguided forays into the hinterland were almost enough to make one renounce ever setting foot in the woods again, but the wildlands beckoned, and each hike led to more competence and new discoveries as the Park revealed its secrets. Later, I did make the trip down the Chéticamp River, not in a boat, but on foot. And I found out that it was just as well we never made it to Chéticamp Lake that first trip, for Fletcher was right: we'd probably have had about as good a chance of making it safely down the river as riding over Niagara Falls in a barrel.

Time and time again I found myself lured back to Cape Breton Highlands National Park with a passion to explore and piece together the different parts of its landscape, curious to see what was around the next bend along a stretch of shoreline, following its rivers like a homing salmon to see where they would wind, searching a way onto ridges to see how the landscape unfolded beyond them, always pushing a little further. There were days on broad barrens when I felt like I could walk forever, with the waste of open country on every side. There were blazing sunsets over the ocean shared with my wife, and dawn awakenings beside wilderness lakes to the sound of water cascading from the antlers of a surfacing moose. With our growing children came diaper changes on the ski trail, and days when "the little ones laughed and leaped and shouted, and all the hills echoed." There was still the odd trip that didn't pan out, those days when no ski wax worked and your pack's shoulder strap broke and you couldn't see where you were going because of the blinding snow and if you got another branch across your freezing face you were going to weep! But the other memories more than compensate for the off-days—the smell of trailing arbutus in the spring and decaying leaves in the fall; ski trips through winter wonderlands where the trees are so caked with snow that no green shows through; evenings of ghost stories and marshmallows beside a campfire; being lulled to sleep by the sound of the surf....

1

Discovering the Park

WHENEVER I DRIVE TO THE PARK, whether to its western or eastern side, the first distant glimpse of the hills of Cape Breton Highlands kindles a feeling of excitement and anticipation. There are two ways to get to the Park by road, both of them along the renowned Cabot Trail. This famous feat of engineering clings to roller-coaster hills beside ocean vistas and pristine forests in a winding 300-kilometre loop around the northern peninsula of Cape Breton Island, traversing three sides of the Park in the process.

Traveling counterclockwise from the village of Baddeck, "the Trail" skirts the shore of St. Ann's Bay as it follows a narrow coastal plain between the edge of the highlands and the sea. After a winding section of road through Wreck Cove that seems to have followed the route of a former cow path, you come around a hairpin turn and abruptly find yourself looking up a steep winding ramp that comprises the road for the next 3 km to the top of Smokey Mountain. The mountain itself is a kind of geographical divide between the region that local inhabitants call "North of Smokey" and the rest of the world. It's from the descent on the other side that you get the first view of the rolling hills of the Cape Breton Highlands National Park spread out in the distance and, through a gap in the mountains, the long, rocky finger of Middle Head jutting out into the Atlantic. You can almost hear the gulls' cry above that sea-girt peninsula, and hear the waves pounding against the rocks. The image evokes the smell of salt air and iodine and spruce.

Equally inviting is the western highway to the Cape Breton Highlands. From the Canso Causeway there are a number of roads you can take to get to that side of the loop, but they eventually coalesce into a single route as they link up one by one with the Cabot Trail.

On this western side of the island the Cabot Trail approaches the Park along the low rolling coastal plain beside the Gulf of St. Lawrence. Beyond the bridge at Margaree Harbour, the sweeping hills that form the edge of the highland plateau remain off in the background at your side, and your gaze is captivated mostly by rocky headlands jutting into the sparkling waters of the Gulf of St. Lawrence. The landscape along here has a windswept feel to it—treeless and grassy. Even some of the houses seem to have been shaped by the wind, as if the truncated corners of their hip roofs have been carved by the sea breezes.

Up ahead lies the French Acadian village of Chéticamp, with the spire of its magnificent stone church piercing the horizon.

Soon after Chéticamp, you become dimly aware that the countryside is changing. A range of high hills and massive cliffs looms in the distance. As the coastal lowlands begin to pinch away between the mountains and the sea, the road turns inland and suddenly steep-sided forested slopes and bare crags rise before you. Another turn in the road and you are looking into a giant cleft in the mountain—the valley of the Chéticamp River—with stone sides so steep you wonder what holds the trees up there. You also start to wonder where the highway goes from here, because the precipitous hills seem to leave no room for a road. A few more minutes and there's the familiar brown and yellow Parks sign.

Within the Canadian national parks system, Cape Breton Highlands represents the Maritime Acadian Highlands Natural Region, one of the 48 Natural Regions into which Canada is divided on the basis of climate, geology, and plant and animal communities. It would be hard to squeeze a more diverse landscape into a thousand square kilometres. Among its rugged hills lie hidden waterfalls, valleys through forest temples, and windswept barrens of moss and heath.

Along the Park's scenic shores, seabirds wheel in the masterless winds, while cruising whales keep them company in the waters offshore. Backed by lagoons, forests or spectacular cliffs, the mood of the coast varies from day to day, hour by hour. Even in winter, when the ocean is packed with ice to the horizon—a frozen desert—the shore itself is often free of snow, and accessible on foot.

In fact, Cape Breton Highlands is by no means just a three-season park; winter offers wonderful opportunities for exploring. By December of most years there is enough snow cover at the higher elevations for cross-country skiing and snowshoeing, and in many years the snow lasts in the Park until late spring, long after it has gone from the rest of the province. I can remember crossing on the Englishtown ferry in the middle of May some years, with not a patch of snow in sight, and having people cast inquiring looks at the skis on the roof racks.

Whether you explore Cape Breton Highlands by car, bicycle or on foot you are bound to be rewarded, especially when you take your time.

Cycling

Its unsurpassed scenery has made the Cabot Trail internationally known as a premier destination for cyclists. My first bicycle trip around "the Trail" was as a teenager on a single speed bike with coaster brakes. Most of us kids then had never seen a multi-speed bike, let alone owned one, but apart from walking and hitchhiking, bicycles were our main means of transportation. Just about the time each year when we should have been studying for final exams we were planning new bike trips or designing improvements to the camping gear that we made mostly from material we scrounged. Those preparations would bring back memories and talk of previous trips—sneaking into the campground at night to socialize, trying to stay one step ahead of the park wardens as they tried to put the run on us. Or hurtling down North Mountain, passing a fish truck (also going down) and wondering what I'd do if my chain came off.

Once, going down French Mountain, one of the carriers

(made from rabbit wire and welding rods) on my bike opened up, and I spent half an hour gathering up cans of food that had rolled under the guardrail and sailed off into the Jumping Brook ravine.

There doesn't seem to be consensus about which way, clockwise or counterclockwise, is the preferred direction to make the circuit of the Park by bike. I have done it in both directions and I'm still undecided. The prevailing winds perhaps dictate a clockwise direction, but on some days the winds can be prevailing from most directions, so what may be a tailwind on one part of the route may be a headwind on the next. Doing the Cabot Trail counterclockwise puts you closer to the outside guardrail— and thus the scenery.

For those contemplating riding the whole loop, a topographic map showing elevation contours will help you in assessing the steepness of hilly sections and in planning rest stops. On days when the spirit is willing but the flesh is weak, I'll sometimes just cycle short sections of the Trail, avoiding the steep grades and taking advantage of the wind direction at the time. (This assumes that you have a vehicle, of course, to take you up the steep parts.) Sections of the highway in the Park that are relatively level with minor hills and dips include the plateau between French and MacKenzie Mountains (about 13 km long), Grande Anse valley (6 km), the plateau on North Mountain (4 km), and the section along the coast between Black Brook and Warren Brook (9 km).

Four of the hiking trails in the Park are also designated for mountain biking: Trous de Saumons, Clyburn Valley, Branch Pond Lookoff, and Freshwater Lake. These are primarily hiking trails described in Chapter 5, and they have some rough places that may not be enjoyed by casual riders.

A number of private companies offer bicycle tours through the Park. These tour companies cater to groups and individuals, with excursions tailored to individual abilities. One local company even provides a shuttle service up the steep inclines of the hills, and a rescue service to cyclists who are stranded by mechanical breakdown. A listing of these companies is available by contacting the Nova Scotia Tourism Information Service at 1-800-565-0000.

Cyclists are required by law in Nova Scotia to wear a helmet.

Canoeing and Kayaking

Because of the small size and steep gradient of the streams in the Park, canoeing opportunities are somewhat limited, but if you do bring your canoe or kayak there are a number of good lakes and ponds. Warren Lake and Freshwater Lake, both on the eastern side of the Park, are easily accessible. Paddling in Warren Lake early in the morning as the rising sun chases the mist from the lake I've come across moose munching on aquatic plants near the shore. On Freshwater Lake I've enjoyed the smell of the nearby ocean breezes and the call of loons, as well as the company of muskrats, beavers and other waterfowl. A short portage from Freshwater Lake will take you into the lagoon inside the barrier beach at Ingonish Harbour.

The Chéticamp River provides a short run during periods of high water, starting from the campground above the highway. In low water you have to wade over the shallow riffles between deeper parts. A couple of kilometres downstream you come to a delta and lagoon, and you are soon within sight of the Petit Étang beach, which divides the lagoon from the ocean. You can also drive to the Petit Étang beach and launch directly into the lagoon from the beach. This is an advantage when the water is low or you don't want to have to paddle upstream against the current to get back to your starting point.

Aucoin Brook, a narrow, meandering tributary of the Chéticamp River draining into the west side of the lagoon at its upper end, provides an interesting paddle through an attractive freshwater marsh. I usually have to wade a bit to get my canoe over a short shallow section upstream of the brook's confluence with the Chéticamp River, but once into the marsh the channel is fairly deep. It's a quiet place where I have seen waterfowl, muskrats and a variety of aquatic plants. The channel meanders in narrow passages through tall bullrushes that grow well over your head.

In fact it's so narrow in places that there's hardly room to paddle, and I've found myself using the bullrushes to pull myself along between the banks. I can get as far as a wooden footbridge that spans the stream before the channel gets too narrow.

Motorboats are not permitted in Park waters.

For experienced canoeists and kayakers the ocean provides spectacular views of the coast with its rugged shoreline, sea stacks, caves and hidden beaches. The shore along the western side of the Park between Petit Étang beach and Corney Brook is accessible from the Cabot Trail in several places, with the longest distance by sea between any two of them being less than 2 km. Along the seaward side of the bluff at Presqu'île I found a shallow cave that I could enter by canoe. Further north, at the foot of the cliffs near Corney Brook, lying half buried on an isolated beach, are the remains of a steam shovel that fell over the mountain years ago during road construction. North of Corney Brook the high red sandstone cliffs are carved into interesting shapes by water and ice. Further along, Jumping Brook, true to its name, leaps off the mountainside into the sea at the mouth of its ravine. Beyond Jumping Brook the walls of rock get higher still, and paddling beneath these towering cliffs is an unforgettable experience. Hundreds of metres above, out of sight on the ridge top, hikers on the Skyline Trail enjoy an eagle's eye view of the waters that I was bobbing on in my tiny craft.

A little further on is another sea cave about 25 metres deep with a high, vaulted ceiling. Sometimes at low tide I've found a cobblestone bar across the entrance where I could beach the canoe and walk part way in, while at other times I could paddle in to the end of the cave. Pieces of pulpwood jammed into a fissure at the apex of the ceiling, high above the water, attest to the violent forces exerted by storm waves when they pound the cave. Inside, the sound of water dripping from the ceiling and the splash of wavelets against the rocks at the entrance seem to get amplified, creating an eerie effect as they reverberate around the cavern walls.

It should be noted that the next access (and therefore take-out) point north of Corney Brook is at Pleasant Bay, 16 km by sea. There are few places to land in an emergency along the way, and none of them are close to any roads. Most of them are bounded by steep mountainsides so that anyone seeking refuge there from bad weather would be virtually stranded until winds and seas abated, which could be several days. Fishing Cove is the only place along that section of shore accessible by a trail, and to get a boat back to a highway by this trail would be a major feat involving a 340 m ascent over 6 km. However, for most kayakers along this coast, Fishing Cove is a planned stop. Pre-registration with the Park is required if you plan to spend the night at Fishing Cove.

On the Atlantic coast of the Park, the best launching and takeout points are the beaches at Neil's Harbour, Black Brook, Broad Cove and Ingonish. The 7 km of coastline between Black Brook and Broad Cove present the longest stretch. There are few opportunities to land easily along here, even though the ocean comes close to the highway in many places.

A further note of caution: The waters off the Park's coast are relatively unprotected from strong, changeable winds and waves, and they are no place for inexperienced boaters. Tidal currents along the Park's shores are negligible, but the currents generated by the counterclockwise flow of the waters of the Gulf of St. Lawrence can be significant, and they become especially strong and more turbulent where they approach the northern tip of the island around Cape St. Lawrence. If you prefer to explore the coastal waters with a local guide, kayak excursions are provided by private companies situated in communities at each "corner" of the Park.

If I don't want to travel any distance along the coast, I sometimes enjoy the pleasure of paddling out from the shore on calm water to look at the mountains and cliffs, or just to rock in the ocean's gentle swell. I take a rope and a large rock from the shore to use as an anchor, to keep from drifting off to Les Îles-de-la-Madeleine if I happen to doze off.

Golf: The Highlands Links

Stanley Thompson was one of the world's great golf course

designers, and Highlands Links, on the Ingonish side of the Park, is usually considered his finest achievement. Ranked best in Canada by *Golf Magazine* and Number One by *Score Magazine*, this 18-hole course extends from the seacoast at Middle Head far into the sheltered Clyburn Valley. The views are so great from every hole that George Knudson, one of Canada's pre-eminent golfers, suggested just leaving your clubs behind and walking the course. Many do.

In 2000, Highlands Links became the second national park golf course to be fully certified by the Audubon Cooperative Sanctuary Program for golf courses. This program is designed to recognize and support golf courses that have worked to ensure a high degree of environmental quality for both people and wildlife.

As Thompson himself wrote: "Nature must always be the architect's model."

Birding

Every spring the woodlands of Cape Breton Highlands come alive with the songs of migrating songbirds, many of which have traveled from as far away as South America. Two hundred thirty species of birds have been recorded in the Park. (A checklist is available at the nature bookstore at the Chéticamp Visitor Centre.) Some of the trails especially popular with birders are Trous de Saumons, Le Buttereau, Corney Brook, Aspy and Warren Lake. The birds' arrival is a good chance to renew identification skills, as their songs become abundant along the Park's trails and roadsides. Often the birds are easier to hear than to see among the trees and shrubbery. I've found that representations of bird songs are helpful in identifying some of the birds. Next time you're walking, see if you can recognize these songs:

A repetitious *Here I am, where are you? Here I am, where are you?* That's the red-eyed vireo.

Teacher, teacher, teacher... (with the accent on the last syllable)—the oven bird.

Zee, zee, zee, zoo, zee or a slower *Trees, trees, murmuring trees* of the black-throated green warbler.

A bright, perky *Sweet, sweet, sweet, little more sweet* is the yellow warbler.

O sweet Canada, Canada, Canada or *Old John Peabody, Peabody, Peabody* is the sound of the white-throated sparrow. The *Canada, Canada, Canada* notes are almost always at a higher pitch than the *O sweet*. However, I've heard a variation of this song in which those notes are lower than the first two. The cadence is the same in each case, but it's as if the birds haven't learned the notes correctly. Perhaps the two different groups of whitethroats sing counterpoint when they get together—a kind of white-throat fugue.

Sweekita, sweekita sweek or *Seekita, seekita seek*: common yellowthroat.

Chick-a-dee-dee-dee: black-capped chickadee.

Cheerily, cheer-up, cheerily... in groups of three or more phrases: robin.

Maids, maids, maids, put on your tea kettle, kettle, kettle or *Madgie, Madgie, Madgie, put on your tea kettle-ettle-ettle* of the song sparrow.

The loud *wick, wick, wick, wick, wick* of the northern flicker reminds me of a car trying to start but not getting any gas.

The call of the red-tailed hawk has been described as an asthmatic squeal, *Keeer-r-r*, slurring downward. Red-tails are often seen or heard soaring above the Park's valleys and mountaintops.

Other birds can be easily recognized not so much by their voices as by the sounds of their courtship rituals. The woods at times reverberate with the drumming of a ruffed grouse as the male proclaims his eligibility through the bird world's equivalent of a lonely hearts column. Leaning back pompously on his fanned tail, the male grouse beats his wings with quick forward and upward strokes. The sound is produced by the cupped wings striking the air. Each time I hear it I wonder if drawing all that attention would also be an invitation for some predator to dine, but the prospect of amour is evidently worth the risk.

Another mysterious sound in the summer sky, especially at dusk or on moonlit nights, is a strange winnowing high overhead.

It's produced by wind rushing through the tail feathers of the male common snipe during its aerial display. The snipe rises on rapid wing beats to some 100 metres high, and then plummets toward the ground at about a 45-degree angle. As its speed increases during the dive, air passing over the outer tail feathers causes them to vibrate, producing a loud tremolo effect. It usually takes me a while to spot the bird because of its fast and unusual flight pattern.

It's not only woodland birds that live in Cape Breton Highlands. Along the coast, seabirds come and go on the rocky ledges and sea stacks, or race along sandy beaches just out of reach of the waves, foraging for food. One of my favourite birds to watch is the northern gannet, and each spring I look forward to seeing the steady procession of these streamlined white seabirds as they migrate along the coast. Their strong, powerful and supremely graceful flight enables them to travel in almost any weather. Rising on the updraft of air that's deflected off the slope of each ocean wave, they skim the wave-tips and glide in a shallow dive to the updraft of the following wave. They can glide for hours like this just above the waves, even against a stiff breeze, while seldom moving their wings.

The gannet's feeding methods are spectacular. Cruising 20 to 30 metres above the water, a gannet sees a fish and, with folded wings, plummets in a nearly vertical dive, sending up a fountain of spray on its impact with the water. The gannet is well equipped for these spectacular plunges. It has no nostril holes, and its upper and lower bills fit tightly together preventing water from being forced into the mouth on impact with the surface. Its streamlined body has a system of air cells between the skin of its neck and shoulders and the underlying muscle, and as the gannet prepares to dive, these cells are inflated to cushion its body when it strikes the water, something like an airbag. Unlike most birds, the gannet has binocular vision—that is, its eyes are positioned so that it can see forward with both, giving it the ability to judge how far the fish are from the surface of the water.

The best places to see gannets are from the higher lookoffs along the coast, such as Cap Rouge or the Skyline Trail on the Park's western side, and Little Smokey on the east.

Botanizing

The Cape Breton Highlands National Park is part of the Maritime Acadian forest region, a transition zone between the eastern North American deciduous forests and the vast boreal forests of the northern hemisphere. That's why plant lovers here have an opportunity to enjoy a mix of northern and southern species that find suitable habitat.

Of course, the region was not always forested at all. During the Ice Age, the Cape Breton Highlands looked like present-day Greenland with barren, unbroken expanses of ice, utterly devoid of plant life. As the ice sheets dwindled, the newly exposed surface of boulders, gravel and clay became available for lichens, grasses and shrubs, but only after considerable time did there develop a soil suitable for trees.

Pollen studies in Cape Breton Highlands tell a story of how the Park's vegetation has changed over time. By boring into the depths of peat bogs researchers obtain core samples of the sediments that built up there. These columns of sediment are examined for pollen grains. Pollen is familiar to anyone who has brushed against a cone-laden branch in spring. The released clouds of yellow dust blow everywhere and often collect as a yellow film on lakes, ponds and clothing. Eventually the grains sink to the bottom where they may be preserved in the sediments for millions of years. Since the shape and texture of a given pollen grain is indicative of the plant species that produced it, it is possible by examining the bog sediments to infer how the Park's vegetation has changed over the centuries.

Gradually, as seeds were blown in from the reservoir of plants south of the ice margin, the Park's tundra vegetation gave way to a boreal forest where fir, birch and spruce predominated. As the climate continued to warm and richer, deeper soils developed, deciduous trees became more plentiful, and the boreal forests were reduced by competition to their present distribution on the plateau.

Today there are three forest regions within the Park: the

Acadian, Boreal, and Taiga. The Acadian forest of mixed hard-woods and conifers grows mostly in the lowlands and on valley slopes. Some of the trees common to the Park's Acadian forest are balsam fir; red, white and black spruce; larch (tamarack); hemlock; white pine; yellow and white birch; red maple; sugar maple; beech; white ash and mountain ash. Decades of logging and farming have eliminated all but remnants of the original Acadian forest, but in a few areas of the Park, it is still possible to see what this forest must have looked like when it fluorished undisturbed. The most notable examples of this old growth forest can be seen in the Grande Anse valley at the Lone Shieling, and along parts of the Aspy hiking trail. Some of the plants here exist at the southern or northern limits of their range, and thus the Park's Acadian forest is important for the study of behaviour of plants as they reach their geographic limits.

The boreal (coniferous) forest and taiga (scrub forest and barrens) occupy the plateau. There are views of these forest types where the highway traverses the plateau along the top of French and North Mountains. Laying my bike beside the road here one day, I jumped across the ditch and pushed through a patch of springy black spruce to find myself standing knee deep in rhodora, with its magenta blooms, and the white flowers of mountain shadbush. A few more paces and I stepped onto a tapestry of golden sedge intertwined with cushions of creamy lichen, dotted with white tufts of cotton grass and the rosy blossoms of bog laurel. The place was like a public garden. Across the far end of a barren moved the dark shape of a browsing moose. Its rich chocolate coat stood out in contrast to its light "leggings." Its antlers, covered in plush velvet, were borne like a regal crown. From the top of a gnarled tamarack tree came the long, plaintive song of a white-throated sparrow.

Each of the three types of forest is accessible to motorists and hikers, and the chapter on hiking trails tells what type you will find as you explore the trails.

A few descendants of the plants that first colonized the landscape around the retreating glaciers persist on small ledges and crannies of the Park's river canyons. Here they are kept cool and moist by seepage from above, or by spray from waterfalls, and are hidden from direct sunlight by the confines of the gorges—critical conditions for their survival. Arctic-alpine plants with names like purple saxifrage and Lapland rosebay inhabit the cliffs of the Chéticamp, Grande Anse and Aspy rivers, for example, where they exist farther south than anywhere else in Canada. Because these populations have developed in isolation from the main parts of their range, they are useful in studies of genetics and provide information about how populations evolve. Plants, as well as birds and animals, will be discussed as we encounter them along the trails in Chapter 5.

Geologizing

Atlantic Canada has a long, complex geological history, but nowhere has it resulted in a more diverse and attractive landscape than in the mountains, valleys and coastlines of Cape Breton Highlands National Park. Bob Raeside, a geologist who has studied the geology of northern Cape Breton, has remarked that the Highlands contain perhaps the greatest variety of igneous rocks in North America. Within the Park are many landforms and features that provide good examples of the processes that shape the landscape, and that are readily seen first hand. Just by following the Cabot Trail through the Park you are driving across parts of three continents and over a billion years of geological history. The fascinating geology of the Park is described in Chapter 3.

Sightseeing by Car

While I'm convinced the best way to see the Park is by shanks' mare, there are times when I just want to vegetate and give my feet a rest. But I can only lie around for so long in this place when there is so much to see. I always feel that I'm missing something. So I get in the car and just go for a drive on the Cabot Trail. It's simply hard to resist one of the finest scenic drives in North America. I might just drive to a lookoff and sit for a while at the edge of some breathtaking ravine, listening to the birds or watching the sun paint the sky as it sinks behind the ocean. On some of the higher coastal lookoffs, like the ones on French Mountain, I've had a thick layer of fog roll in beneath me, completely obliterating the landscape below, and leaving me and the surrounding hilltops isolated above a sea of cotton.

You never know when or where you might see a white-tailed deer, a fox or a coyote crossing the highway. If you're really lucky, you may see a bear or even a lynx. I've seldom made a circuit of the Park without at least one sighting of its largest resident, the moose, feeding on the vegetation along the roadside.

You can even go birding by car. Cape Breton Island has one of the largest nesting populations of bald eagles east of the Rockies, and their distinctive white head and majestic flight make the great birds easy to spot soaring along the coastal sections of the Cabot Trail. The large population in Cape Breton has permitted a program of translocating the birds to the northeastern United States, where they have been successfully reestablished.

One calm summer evening I was drifting along the western shore of the Park in my canoe, making my way back from Fishing Cove. High red sandstone cliffs towered above me, turning redder as the sun got lower. The sea was like mercury, reflecting the blue and gold and crimson of the sky and sunset. The only sounds were the splash of my paddle and the wheezy *peeeeee* of a black guillemot swimming on the surface ahead of me. As I glided toward it, the little puffin-like seabird ducked its head into the water, making sure it was safe to dive, and with a quick beat of its wings disappeared under the surface. There was a momentary glimpse of its white wing patches as it used its wings to "fly" through the water. It bobbed back up a little distance away but I was still heading for it. This time when I got too close it ran along the surface of the water until it could lift off, and with its bright red legs trailing behind, it circled around me a couple of times and landed again, satisfied that I was no threat.

Paddling close to the cliffs I could see down through the water to where rock crabs and sea stars rested on the bottom. As I drifted around a sea stack a startled great blue heron lifted off a barnacle-covered rock and flapped away in slow motion toward Chéticamp Island. I paddled back out from the shore, into the empty, glimmering expanse toward the horizon where I could get a better view of the hills behind the cliffs. I've heard the term "aquellae" suggested to describe those myriad flashes of light created by the reflections of sunlight on the dimpled surface of the water, and that the sea was "brinkling" when it did this. The scene was so magical I wanted to stay out on the water as long as I could.

The smell of wood smoke from the campfires at the Corney Brook campground drifted over the water, and I saw people gathering on the bank above the shore to watch the sunset. Some of them were pointing seaward. At what? People were beckoning to others, and as more people gathered to look I stood up in the canoe to try to see what they were looking at. The trail of light on the water leading towards the sun made it difficult.

Then I saw them—pilot whales! The black arcs of their backs broke the surface about 300 metres away. Again and again they broached, sometimes singly, sometimes two or more at a time. There must have been dozens of them. Suddenly, directly in front of me, not six metres away, the bulbous forehead of a whale shot up at a low angle out of the water and then plowed back in, followed by the long gentle arc of the glistening body. I sat down in the canoe, grasping the gunwales, wondering what to do. I had paddled pretty far from shore, intending to drift back in with the slight sea breeze. Behind me there came a hissing sound, as of a slight turmoil in the water, and I turned in time to see the black, rubbery dorsal surface and the fin slip beneath the waves.

They were all around me. And they seemed to be having so much fun, as if they were taking part in a sort of marine loppet. There was a mother and her calf, the two of them broaching and diving in unison. The whales seemed benign and playful with their permanent carefree smiles, and they showed no particular interest in the canoe—but what if one of them was to accidentally surface under the canoe? In any case, if I was going to be upset it was too late to do anything about it at that point, so I just sat and watched the show. In the end, they passed by with what seemed almost deliberate courtesy by not crowding the canoe, and once again it was just me and the guillemot floating in the twilight.

As I said earlier, I can never make up my mind which direction, clockwise or counterclockwise, is best for driving through the Cape Breton Highlands. I'd recommend giving yourself enough time to travel it both ways. The views are different in each direction, so it's like traveling two different Parks. An advantage of starting at the western entrance is that you can begin your visit at the Chéticamp Visitor Centre, where you can orient yourself with a display of slides and videos about the Park. The Visitor Centre also houses Atlantic Canada's largest nature bookstore with a wide selection of field guides and maps, as well as an interesting collection of books about Cape Breton Island.

The much smaller stone welcome centre at the Ingonish entrance to the Park has no displays or bookstore, but the staff there will provide you with information about campgrounds, evening programs and the surrounding communities.

A few driving tips should be mentioned. The steep descents on the mountains can be hard on brakes. The constant friction can lead to overheating, and the smell of hot brakes often permeates the air on these slopes. The remedy is to put the vehicle in a lower gear and use the engine to retard your speed. By applying the brakes only when needed you lower the chance of overheating.

Moose often cross or travel upon the roads in the Park, quite unheeding of traffic. You really have to watch your speed and be prepared to stop suddenly, especially at night. You sometimes see the dim yellow-green reflection of their eyes, but you won't even see that if their stern end is toward you. In the winter, some moose discover it's a lot easier to travel on the highway than in the snow-filled woods, and I've come across them kneeling on their forelegs licking road salt from the pavement. It's fairly common to see their urine stains and piles of dung on the roadway some mornings, before the traffic erases them. These signs, as well as tire skid marks here and there along the pavement, should serve as reminders to conduisez prudement.

When stopping to take pictures or to watch wildlife, it's in everyone's best interest to pull completely off the pavement, as vehicles stopped on the highway can pose a traffic hazard.

These cautions are not meant to scare you—well, okay, they are a little bit—but not enough to keep you off the road. But if you would prefer to let someone else drive so that you can watch the scenery, there are commercial companies in the region that offer guided van tours and walking tours in the Park. One of them even specializes in moose watching.

Interpretive Programs and Community Events

A good introduction to the Cape Breton Highlands National Park is through the lively and informative interpretive events and programs scheduled both daytime and evenings during July and August. Presented by Park staff, they cover subjects from birds to beavers, plant life, local history and the stars. Schedules are available at the Visitor Centres and kiosks.

Salmon dinners, lobster suppers, Celtic and Acadian concerts, festivals and celebrations take place throughout the year in the villages adjacent to the Park. Notices of these events are displayed on bulletin boards throughout the communities, and Visitor Services staff can tell you more about them.

Weather

Wherever you go in the Park, one thing that will govern your activities is the weather. Given that several major air masses converge on the Atlantic coastal region, the constant jostling among them guarantees a seasonal, daily and even hourly variability in the weather of Cape Breton Highlands. Add to this the influence of the local topography, and the fickleness of the weather is sure to confound forecasters and provide lots of variety for weather watchers. Just when you think you're about to become mildewed from several consecutive days of rain, the weather can change and there will be hardly another drop for the rest of the summer.

The prevailing winds in the region are westerlies from continental North America, but with Cape Breton stuck out in the Atlantic as it is, the temperatures of its winds are moderated by the ocean, and therefore they don't usually reach the extremes of more continental areas. On a seasonal basis, winds blowing over the cool coastal waters delay the arrival of spring compared to more western parts of Nova Scotia so that in some years it can be well into June before it feels comfortable in shirtsleeves, and only the hardiest swimmers venture into the ocean before July. At the other end of the summer, though, long after the days begin to shorten, the influence of ocean currents extends the warm weather through September and into October.

"What's the weather like here in winter? Is there much snow?" It's hard to say without asking, "Which winter?" because it varies from year to year. I know one thing, though: If they ever make snow shovelling an Olympic sport, there will be a lot of medal contenders from the North of Smokey crowd. You know you're in snow country when you hear people comparing the performance and handling qualities of different styles of snow shovels as if they were talking about the merits of different brands of fly rods. In any given winter there is a marked difference between the weather in the lowlands and that on the highland plateau, where early snows in October and late storms in May occasionally leave unequipped cars temporarily stranded on mountaintops. The raw winds of November ("no shade, no shine, no butterflies, no bees, no fruits, no flowers, no leaves, no birds—November!") usually bring the season's first wet flurries. Yearly snowfall on the plateau is often the highest in the Maritimes, but periods of rain and thaw during the winter keep snow depths substantially below the total snowfall. When hiking in the backcountry, I've often come across patches of snow in July left over from the winter.

An interesting phenomenon on the western side of the Park—especially to people camping in tents!—is the occurrence of a strong southeasterly wind known locally as a suête, which sometimes sweeps down the slopes of the plateau with hurricane force. The severity of these winds, which can reach speeds of 200 km an hour, is influenced by the configuration of the wall of hills behind the coastal plain from Margaree Harbour to Petit Étang. Many of the houses in the Chéticamp area have shuttered windows on their eastern side because of these winds, and residents move their cars to the leeward side of their houses prior to a suête to prevent them from being sandblasted. In St. Joseph du Moine you'll see a few very old houses attached to the barns, an arrangement that allowed people to tend and milk their animals in the worst weather without going outdoors.

A particularly severe suête occurred one evening in March of 1993 when the wind blew in picture windows of several houses, and in one house opened cupboards and distributed the contents, including a bag of flour, around the inside of the house. Part of the roof of the hospital in Chéticamp was blown away, and the metal flagpole in front of the Chéticamp Visitor Centre was bent over. As the wind increased throughout the evening, it seemed that every window in my house was rattling. Around midnight, as I lay awake listening to the house creaking and the wind howling, I thought of Byron's

And this is in the night, most glorious night.
Thou wert not meant for slumber! Let me be
A sharer of thy fierce and far delight—
A portion of the tempest and of thee!

I decided to go for a walk.

I started out along the highway from Petit Étang and headed toward the Rigwash Valley. I was doing all right tacking along a fairly protected stretch of road until I came to the Chéticamp River. There I seemed to enter a wind tunnel created by the river valley and was swept off my feet as I tried to cross the bridge. The only way to make headway was to hang on to the guardrail with my arms and resist being blown out horizontally like a party streamer. Things were flying through the air—trees perhaps, possibly small mammals, even moose antlers. I'm not sure. I couldn't see very well in the dark. At one point I saw what must have been the top of a spruce tree bounding toward me in a zigzag course like a giant tumbleweed. It must have snapped off a tree somewhere up ahead. With visions of being swept up like a piece of lint in a brush, I managed to zig when it zagged, and continued on my way.

Curiously, the further I got into the valley of the Rigwash the less force the wind seemed to have. Although it just screamed overhead near the summits of the ridges on either side, the air in the valley was relatively still, and at times it was actually hard to feel which direction it was coming from. Things picked up again, however, when I reached the other end. Where the valley of Jerome Brook makes its exit beside La Grande Falaise, the wind was being funnelled through the gap and it nearly took my breath away.

I don't recall what time I blew back into my yard that night, but the return trip was just as exhilarating.

Apart from prolonged periods of rain, perhaps the most frustrating weather in the Park occurs when low clouds envelope the mountaintops and hide the views. On rainy days, though, I've taken pleasure in walking along the shore or on some protected woodland trail. Even on those wild days when no one but a Viking would be out, it's interesting to take a drive to a lookoff and watch the squalls trace patterns or raise waterspouts on the surface of the ocean, or feel the power of the wind as it buffets your car and flings chunks of foam up the faces of the cliffs. In cloudy weather there can be dramatic skies and cloud formations when the weather begins to break and the fog swirls around the mountaintops and rolls up the hillsides and valleys. Walk along one of the cobble beaches in the Park during a storm and listen to the hoarse rumbling of boulders being rolled back and forth in the tumultuous surf. After a rainy walk it's nice to come back to dry out—ah, the feel of dry socks—in one of the kitchen shelters, making new acquaintances with people from other parts, and trading stories of Park experiences around a crackling wood stove. Or just hunker down with that book you packed for a rainy day, the one you never seem to have time to read.

If you want the weather forecast for the Highlands region in a nutshell, phone the weather office at (902) 564-7357 or check with the Visitor Services people.

2

Before the Park
A Short History

ESTABLISHED IN 1936, Cape Breton Highlands was the first national park in the Atlantic region. This chapter is a brief account of the human settlement of the Park area and how the site came to be chosen as one of Canada's national treasures.

The First Inhabitants

Caribou weren't the only species that followed retreating ice sheets into the newly vegetated areas in what is now Cape Breton Highlands. Ten thousand years ago the abundance of game animals in northern Cape Breton maintained a steady flow of small bands of early aboriginal people, called Paleo-Indians. Spear points discovered in 1975 on Ingonish Island, near the southeastern corner of the Park, are evidence of their presence. Ingonish Island was important to these earliest humans for its outcrop of andesite, a type of volcanic rock suitable for making stone tools, and thus served as a prehistoric quarry site and workshop. During the lowered sea levels at that time Ingonish Island was likely connected to the mainland by dry land.

As the climate continued to change, the tundra-like landscape of Paleo-Indian times gave way to boreal forests, and later to mixed hardwoods. As the glaciers thawed, rising sea levels gradually drowned much of the land along the coast. Besides the changes in the land, the aboriginal population also changed, from people who were primarily big game hunters of the tundra to people that were increasingly adapted to the coast and who relied extensively on its abundant marine resources. These people, known as the Maritime Archaic Indians, followed a pattern of seasonal migration between the coast in summer with its fish, shellfish, seals, walrus and sea birds, and the interior plateau and valleys in winter, where they hunted caribou.

These small, nomadic bands of Maritime Archaic Indians left few traces of other aspects of their culture, such as housing or their language. What became of them is almost as mysterious as their origins. All we know is that the Maritime Archaic culture disappeared as a recognizable entity some 3500 years ago and was replaced by that of the Mi'kmaq Indians. The stone weapons and tools characteristic of the earlier people were no longer made. Evidence suggests that swordfish, which seemed to have been a mainstay of the Maritime Archaic diet in the area, became scarcer and the use of shellfish became more prominent. Whether these users of shellfish were the same people as the early Maritime Archaic Indians is a matter of dispute. The results of studies in the fields of archaeology, linguistics, genetics, and the study of human skeletons have so far been inconclusive in establishing a historical continuity between the two cultures. In any event, sometime late in the period preceding European contact in the late 1500s, there developed a distinctive Mi'kmaw culture.

The Mi'kmaq

The Mi'kmaq were nomadic hunters and gatherers but were more dependent on the sea than their predecessors. Their lives shifted with the seasons as they moved between the coast and the interior. Birchbark canoes, sleds and toboggans were used for transport. In winter they hunted beaver, otter, caribou and bear, using bows, arrows and snares. They hunted moose by stalking and running them down in deep snow.

Nicholas Denys, an accurate recorder of both natural and cultural phenomena in 17th-century Nova Scotia, mentions "so great a quantity of wild geese, ducks, and brant...that it is not believable," and that other birds "rose into the air [and] made a cloud so thick that the rays of the sun could scarcely penetrate through it." In spite of this seasonal bounty, though, severe winters often meant hardship and starvation.

Before the Park: A Short History

Although the coasts, rivers and forests all played a part in the Mi'kmaw economy, up to ninety percent of their food came from the sea. And although hunting in the interior was considered a more prestigious activity than fishing, it occupied far less time and provided far less to the diet. In late winter, when the shore and river ice began to break up, the Mi'kmaq moved to the bays, estuaries, coves and river mouths where they harvested fish, shellfish, waterfowl, eggs, seals, walrus, and occasionally harpooned small whales from canoes. Fishing was by hook-and-line and harpoon, and large fish weirs were constructed near spawning sites to catch migratory fish such as salmon and eels.

The Mi'kmaq of prehistoric times were scattered in very small bands over a large area. The size of these social groups—they could hardly be called "settlements"—varied with the season. Winter camps were made up of small groups of several related families, while in summer more abundant resources allowed bands of several hundred individuals to form. Housing consisted of portable bark or hide-covered wigwams, reflecting the need for mobility.

Human occupation of Cape Breton extends back for thousands of years, and although the aboriginal peoples seem to have left few traces of their existence in the region that later became the Park, there is no doubt that they followed the caribou trails of the highlands, fished its rivers, and sustained themselves with the resources of its bays and estuaries. Through the centuries the region's inhabitants adjusted to dramatic climatic change, for example, as well as significant technological developments. At some unknown time in the past, the Maritime Archaic people became adjusted to life along the coast and developed a technology for harpooning seals, walrus, swordfish and perhaps even small whales. The technique for making clay pots was not invented in the Mi'kmaw area but was imported from elsewhere, probably the upper St. Lawrence, from where it passed eastward into the Maritimes. There is evidence, as well, that the culture of the inhabitants was influenced by the arrival of new aboriginal groups from the south. None of these things, however, would have as great an effect upon the people and the land as the coming of strangers from Europe.

European Settlement

Historical references to voyages by Norse sailors along Cape Breton's shores in the 10th century have long existed. Among the first of the European explorers to leave an account of landfall in North America was John Cabot, an Italian navigator in the service of England. Whether his first glimpse of the New World was of the highlands of Cape Breton or Newfoundland will be forever disputed by people on both sides of the Cabot Strait, but his voyage of discovery in 1497 is commemorated at Cabot Landing, a few kilometres north of the Cape Breton Highlands National Park. And, of course, the name given to the Cabot Trail perpetuates his memory.

By the 1500s the seemingly inexhaustible fisheries of the North Atlantic coastal waters were attracting European fishing fleets. Basque and English fishermen used the eastern coast of the Park for drying their catches, coming ashore to erect frames of poles upon which to sun-dry their harvest. In 1525 the Portuguese attempted to found a colony at Ingonish, but being from a country that's just a stone's throw from the sunny Mediterranean, they abandoned it probably due to harsh winters. For almost two centuries following the departure of the Portuguese, the only other inhabitants of Cape Breton remained the Mi'kmaq and occasional groups of European fishermen, while the whole northern peninsula remained devoid of any permanent European settlement.

France established a fishing settlement at Ingonish in 1729 as an outpost of the fortress town of Louisbourg, but it was burned by a combined British-New England fleet in 1745, just prior to the fall of Louisbourg. The site of an early burial ground from this era was discovered near Number Four green during the construction of the Highlands Links golf course.

In 1755 the British expelled the Acadian French from their lands in mainland Nova Scotia. Some of the exiled Acadians eventually found their way to the Chéticamp area where they farmed and supplied fish to Huguenots, French-speaking merchants from the English Jersey Islands. More French immigrants came to Cape Breton following the French Revolution of 1789. Today, more than 200 years later, the Chéticamp area retains its distinct Acadian culture and Acadian French is still the language of daily life amidst its mainly English-speaking neighbours. Descendents of these early immigrants lived at Cap Rouge along the western side of what is now Cape Breton Highlands National Park until the 1930s, when the federal government expropriated their homes in order to establish the Park.

In the early 1800s from across the sea, Scottish and Irish immigrants came to the region that would become Cape Breton Highlands. In the Highlands and Islands thousands of Scottish crofters were uprooted and dispersed, their humble homes often burned behind them, to make room for more lucrative sheep and hunting estates. Many of them found passage to the shores of Nova Scotia, and around 1820 families of these immigrants began to homestead in Pleasant Bay and the Grande Anse valley, supporting themselves by fishing and subsistence farming. The influence of the Gaelic language can still be heard in the speech of their descendants.

Also around 1820 about a dozen English, Irish and Dutch immigrants became the first permanent settlers in Ingonish. Some of the land that they occupied, such as Warren Lake, Clyburn Valley and Middle Head, were later taken over by the Park. A few people had begun to settle along the shore of Aspy Bay— including American Loyalists—and with the influx of Highlanders after 1800 the backlands around Big Intervale were settled.

Neil's Harbour was the last of the communities around the Park to be settled, mainly by Newfoundland immigrants of English descent in the 1860s. They were encouraged to settle in Cape Breton by merchants who promised to buy their fish. Today you can still detect a trace of Old World inflection in the speech of Neil's Harbour's inhabitants.

Writing around 1880, Hugh Fletcher gave the following description of the Highlands region: "The northern...district is high, sterile and uninhabited, except at certain points on the coast and for some miles up the rivers flowing into Pleasant Bay, St. Lawrence, Aspy, Ingonish and St. Ann's Bays. Outside these settlements this northern region is but little known, being intersected by wild, rocky gorges, through which streams with numerous falls flow from the barrens, marshes and small lakes in which they originate."

Fit terrain for a national park perhaps, but hardly the description of an easy place to live. Consequently, people's lives in these remote parts were oriented to the coast, and lands along the shore were settled first. Here at least they were close to a major source of sustenance, and some communication was possible by water.

Fishing became the mainstay of their livelihoods. Before the advent of the internal combustion engine fishing stations and shanties were established on remote parts of the coast in order to be close to the fishing grounds. As the population grew into the 20th century, the rolling lowlands and intervales became dotted with small, multi-crop and subsistence farms. With few links to the outside world, or even with each other, the communities by necessity developed an independent way of life. Roads in northern Cape Breton were non-existent up to the late 1800s, so scattered settlements met their need for self-sufficiency with the construction of grist mills, saw mills, lime kilns, carding mills, tanneries, forges, churches and schools.

Early Transportation

The isolation between communities, and even between neighbours, manifested the need for greater ease of travel between them. The first overland links of any kind between communities were only narrow trails blazed from one settlement to another. All traveling had to be done on foot or on horseback, over mountains or bridgeless rivers, or by boat from bay to bay. Travel by water along the rugged coast was risky at best, given the unpredictability of the weather, and was only possible during those months when there was no ice. Shipwrecks were common. In fact, some years are remembered according to the bounty that washed ashore from shipwrecks: Year of the Flour, Year of the Butter, Year of the Rum, etc.

In 1850 a path was cleared from St. Ann's Bay to Bay St. Lawrence, and another one started from Chéticamp to Pleasant Bay. In 1893 a trail was blazed eastward from Pleasant Bay to the Aspy valley. The blazed path eventually became wide enough to permit passage of a horse and rider, but these paths were extremely difficult for those on foot or horseback and they were too rough to accommodate wagons or carriages. Travel during the winter could be especially brutal.

One spring a woman from Middle River, Victoria County, came to Pleasant Bay to visit friends. She had walked over the mountain trail from Chéticamp, visited for a few days and then decided to travel on to Cape North. She reached Big Intervale late in the afternoon but found the North Aspy River too high and swift to cross. With night approaching, it was too late to turn back to Pleasant Bay. Her cries for help were heard by a family living nearby but in the darkness it was impossible to cross the river. The next morning they did manage to get across but were met with the grim sight of the woman frozen to the ground.

An account of another fatal journey in that era was carried by the *Sydney Post*: "On the 13th of December [c. 1865], Mrs. Mary Ann Brown [with her husband and son-in-law] left Ingonish for Cape North to visit her sick daughter there. On the road the party was overtaken by a violent snowstorm. At a point called Black Brook, Mrs. Brown, overcome by fatigue and exposure, lost all power to continue the journey and died in the presence of her two weary companions. This is another evidence of the need of a house of refuge on the lonely dismal road that the traveler follows on his way from Ingonish to Cape North." Today, the beautiful Mary Ann Falls on the eastern side of the Park bears her name.

Tragedies like this prompted the government to establish and subsidize a number of rest stations, called halfway houses, at strategic points along the trails. A halfway house was built in 1868 on the road from Ingonish to Cape North a couple of kilometres from Neil's Harbour, which had been founded the same year. From about 1888 to 1925 halfway houses were also operated in Fishing Cove and at Cap Rouge, on the western side between Chéticamp and Pleasant Bay. Little seems to be known about the latter two, but the one at Neil's Harbour was a going concern until 1912. Besides the house there was a barn, stable, pig house, milk house and a garden. Typical of homes in the area, the house was described by one traveler as "just what a refuge should be—warm, clean and hospitable. The door opens into a large kitchen with a generous stove on one side and a floor that shines from much scrubbing. The MacPhersons keep the place and have for many a year."

These refuges were invaluable over the years by providing food and shelter to the weary traveler as well as a rest and changeover point for the local mail carriers, which greatly facilitated postal service. "The sight of the halfway house cheers the weary wayfarer more than language can express," commented a school inspector in 1891. Without them more lives would have been lost on the desolate trails of northern Cape Breton.

Improvements in these trails came slowly. In 1881 one disgruntled traveler reported, "From the halfway house to Black Brook is nearly five miles. The most of this road, if called a road, is over a low rocky bottom over which flows a copious stream of water at nearly all seasons of the year, excepting a short space of dry season. During summer this is one of the worst roads in the dominion. It is particularly dangerous at this time of year [December] for man or beast, as most of the corduroy bridges are broken down and a traveler cannot see where to put his foot."

The trails were eventually widened to accommodate wagons. They were crude at first, often not much more than paths with notches cut in the larger stumps to let the hubs of the wagon wheels pass. An American visitor traveling to Cape North in 1886 wrote, "The road was a bridle path partly over swamps, partly up and down the beds of stony brooks. We were on top of the barren plateau of Cape Breton, a mossy, burned, desolate region where bare, bleached skeletons of trees shake in the wind and the huckleberry alone struggles over the rocks. It is wearisome to pick your way for miles in such ground, jumping from bog to bog, stone to stone, or walking single poles laid as bridges over peat holes. The region, of course, is uninhabited excepting the halfway house."

Although residents pressed for improvements, isolation continued. Some communities were serviced by small coastal schooners and, in the 1880s, by steamers. By the last quarter of the 19th century transportation had improved to the point where people were able to visit the area for reasons other than business. A small trickle of tourists began to arrive and the scenic attractions of the northern part of the island became more and more known.

Improvements continued to be made to the road system in the region partly because of local needs and partly out of a desire to attract tourists. But improvements were slow in coming. A traveler over Smokey wrote: "We had rounded one shoulder of the mountain where the edge of the road had slipped down four or five hundred feet into a brook bed, leaving only room for a wagon to pass between the unguarded edge of the ravine and the gravel bank which rose from the road on its other side. A horse having already plunged down there, I, even on my own feet, did not like the sensation of passing this spot."

Another wayfarer, M. W. Morley, in 1905 described the route beyond Mary Ann Falls: "Soon...the road dwindled to a mere track where the horse waded up to his middle in grass, everlasting, and goldenrod, and finally plunged into the dismal swamp that crosses the country here. We laboured for several miles through as desolate a region as one need care to know. It was for the most part an alder-choked swamp, the road cut through a solid wall of gloomy green, the wheels oftentimes hub-deep in mud, while stones in the ruts constantly canted the wagon to one side or the other. We named this charming road the Melancholy Way of the Alders. We met no one, and so we shall never know what would have happened if we had, in that narrow alley where one could scarcely have pulled out of the deep ruts even if there had been any place to pull to."

Most of the roadwork in the 1800s had been done by voluntary labour, and for about 20 years at the beginning of the 1900s statute labour was required of every man under the age of 60, according to the value of his property. Pressure for improvements continued but changes were slow.

Doctors often had to risk their lives to reach patients north of Smokey. Since the road could not accommodate more than one vehicle at a time, it was the custom to stop at the telegraph station on the south side of the mountain and contact the northern station to indicate one's intention to cross Smokey. Some motorists were in the habit of cutting a spruce tree at the summit and tying it to the back of the car so that the branches dragged all the way down the mountain to prevent the car from speeding out of control.

The Cabot Trail

At the urging of local municipal governments, a push to complete a highway loop connecting the northern communities began in 1924. Gangs of men using picks, shovels and dynamite—and later gas shovels and jackhammers—began to hack out a roadbed through the difficult terrain. The final link over North Mountain was completed in 1932, but the road still remained an adventure. As one writer reported: "Nightmares of blown tires or mechanical failures haunted the squeamish travelers as they inched their way around hairpin turns and struggled up steep mountainous grades. Speed was out of the question. Five to seven miles an hour was normal for the Cap Rouge section, while at best only twelve to fifteen miles an hour was possible." One resident remembers two men and two women going up Cap Rouge mountain. One woman was running ahead of the car to check out the curves, and there were two men running behind the car with big rocks in their hands in case the car stalled and began to roll backwards.

Still, the Cabot Trail eliminated the isolation that had characterized the region for generations, not only between the people of northern Cape Breton and the rest of the world, but among the scattered communities themselves.

The Cape Breton Highlands National Park Is Born

In the early 1900s Nova Scotians were campaigning for a

On the Old Cabot Trail

TOP: **Farms in the Rigwash Valley, 1933, before the Park was created; right background is Le Buttereau.** BOTTOM: **Workmen clear a rock fall on the western side of the Cabot Trail.**

TOP: **Plank road on Smokey Mountain.** CENTRE: **North Mountain, 1934.** BOTTOM: **Looking south from Cape Smokey. With the completion of the roadway between Cape North and Pleasant Bay, the Cabot Trail was officially opened in 1932.**

national park in their province. Various sites throughout Nova Scotia were proposed, including the northern part of Cape Breton Island. By 1934 the number of potential sites had been reduced to four—northern Cape Breton, a site at Blomidon overlooking Grand Pré and the Annapolis Valley, a site near Yarmouth at the western end of the province, and the Louisbourg-Gabarus area. R. W. Cautley, an engineer with the Department of the Interior, toured all four sites to assess their potential for the creation of a national park. In the end, he strongly recommended Cape Breton with its "outstanding scenic attractions of rugged coast line and mountain grandeur which is the best of its type within the Province of Nova Scotia." He wrote: "The approaches to the Park site pass through magnificent scenery of an entirely different kind, which is unsurpassed anywhere and which adds greatly to the value of the site itself as a world-famous tourist resort."

Cautley saw the Cabot Trail as one of the advantages of the Cape Breton site. He envisioned that, "A highway could be built along the coast which, in my opinion, would be the most spectacular marine drive that I have ever seen in any part of Canada. In full view of the sea and the rugged coast, it would be located high up on the cliffs in places and at others, would follow the grassy slopes at the entrance of picturesque valleys."

Cautley also felt that the establishment of a national park would provide economic benefits at least as great as any that might be derived from the development of the site's natural resources. "It will be a source of pride," he said, "as well as profit, to the people of Nova Scotia."

It is worth noting that Cautley speaks little of the interior, or of animals and plants. He was thinking of an automotive tourists' park rather than preservation of an extraordinary landscape and its creatures. But the establishment of the Park helped to preserve the region—and regardless of Cautley's plan we are the benefactors. Two years after his survey, on June 23, 1936, Cape Breton Highlands National Park was created.

For the people who lived within its boundaries at Cap Rouge, Pleasant Bay, Big Intervale and Ingonish, the establishment of the Park brought mixed blessings. While the Park contributed to economic development in northern Cape Breton, and provided financial compensation and employment to the families involved, the expropriation of the homes and the forced departure of their inhabitants remains a source of bitterness. "It's given a lot of employment to a lot of people," said Leona Dunphy of Ingonish whose family's farm was taken over. "Most of the ones who lost their property to the Park were more or less guaranteed jobs, and even their children and grandchildren have jobs because of the takeover. But on the other side...a lot of fishermen hauled their boats up on the beach, and they rotted there. It made some dependent on the Park. They lost the independence that they had."

A golf course now occupies the site of her old home, and campgrounds and other Park facilities occupy some of the other farmlands taken over by the Park. In places where the old clearings are being reclaimed by the forest, the mossy stone cellars, wells and stone walls remind us of the joys, grief, hardships and simplicity of another era.

As the Cabot Trail assumed new prominence a number of changes were made in order to avoid excessive grades on some portions. The steep, precarious route up the valley of Canadian Brook to the top of French Mountain was abandoned in favour of the present highway route up the valley of Jumping Brook. (Parts of these old abandoned roads are still passable on foot and are described at the end of the chapter on hiking trails.) During the late 1940s and early 1950s the Trail between North Ingonish and Neil's Harbour was relocated and rebuilt. Prior to this, the road followed the inland route past Mary Ann Falls; the new route is within sight of the ocean for most of the way.

In 1952 the first sort of guardrail was placed along the edge of the most dangerous parts of the Trail and was built of wooden posts six feet apart. Some sections were paved in the mid-fifties, and on July 18, 1961, "Completion of Paving" ceremonies were held near Corney Brook which were attended by more than 500 people. I can still remember my sister and I, as kids, hanging out the car window, urging Dad to drive closer to the logs that served as a guardrail so that we could look down into the ravines, while our frantic mother tried to make us get back in. Whenever we met another vehicle on the unpaved portions we had to wind the windows up in order to keep the dust out.

Today the Cabot Trail is a safe, well-maintained highway. In spite of its exciting hills and hairpin turns, mishaps are few. Still, for some, the excitement can be a little too much. Wardens and park attendants occasionally receive calls to help people stopped on the mountaintops, too overwhelmed at the prospect of another white-knuckled descent to continue. One day I came upon a car stopped in the middle of the lane near the top of North Mountain—over the crest of the hill, aiming down. The terrified driver had her foot on the brake, a death-grip on the wheel, the emergency brake was set, and she refused to go another inch. I persuaded her to get into the back seat and drove her car to the bottom, then hitched a ride back up. The car had Oregon license plates, and I have no idea how she got over the Rockies.

Rigwash Valley and La Grande Falaise

3

Geology

The Park's Landscape
and How It Got That Way

ONE EVENING, after a day of hiking on the western side of the Park, I found myself lingering on the summit of some high crags. As the setting sun deepened the orangey-pink colour of the rock, I thought, "I've seen pink rock like this on the other side of the Park, and yet the rock is not continuous from one side of the Park to the other. How is it that there are different kinds and colours of rock in between, and how do all the different rocks get to be positioned beside or on top of one another?" In only a few hundred vertical metres I had gone from flaky, layered sediments near the shore, past dark bands of what looked like hardened lava on the lower part of the face, to the pink crystalline stuff that I was leaning against at the moment. For that matter, why are there mountains and valleys, highlands and lowlands, sandy beaches in one place, rocky beaches or no beaches in others?

There are people whose eyes would glaze over if you were to suggest that the story written in rocks was something to get excited about. But it's hard to travel around in the outdoors without failing to notice the great variety of things—plants, birds, rocks—that are so lavishly bestowed all around us. And eventually, you want to know their names and, if you're curious enough, where they come from and what they do. In the case of rocks, the inevitable consequence of this for me was an interest in geology.

Rock forms the main features of the landscape of Cape

Breton Highlands National Park: canyons to lose yourself in, pinnacles to head to, and the variation in relief that contributes so much to the Park's magnificent scenery. To some extent the bedrock even determines the kinds of plants that grow there.

The Diverse Origins of Atlantic Canada

The further down into the earth you go, the hotter it gets. In the nether regions, 50 km or so, the temperature gets hot enough to partially melt rock. Some of this heat was generated when the solid materials that formed the planet were crunched together by gravity, but today the heat is generated primarily from the radioactive decay of certain elements inside the earth. The continual release of heat from the earth's interior has created a band of partially molten rock called the asthenosphere, from 50 to 250 km beneath the earth's surface. Below this mobile layer, increasing pressure overcomes the effect of temperature, and the rock becomes solid again. Above the mobile layer are rigid bands of rock which, for the sake of simplicity, we will call the crust. The crust is fractured into segments called plates.

Nova Scotia is a composite of continental plate fragments that were formed in different parts of the globe. These fragments—or terranes—actually wandered over the earth's surface until they were plastered against one another when they collided.

The oldest rocks in the province make up the northwest tip of Cape Breton. Within the Park they are found on the top of the western ascent of North Mountain. These rocks, known as the Blair River Terrane, are over a billion years old. It's believed that they originated as sediments that eroded from the Canadian Shield, the ancient continental core of North America. Later, during a period of plate collisions, the sediments were metamorphosed as they were incorporated into a huge mountain that was thrown up along the eastern edge of the shield. In time, the mountains eroded. The rocks of the Blair River Terrane are remnants of the roots of these eroded mountains.

Along the Cabot Trail from the Park entrance at Ingonish to Warren Brook, and at Middle Head, you can find rocks that came from a different part of the earth. They are the roots of an eroded volcanic island chain, similar to the islands that make up the Caribbean today. They once lay thousands of kilometres away in an ancient sea, and had been formed by the collision between crustal plates. When a continental and an oceanic plate collide, the former usually overrides the latter, forcing the leading edge of the oceanic plate

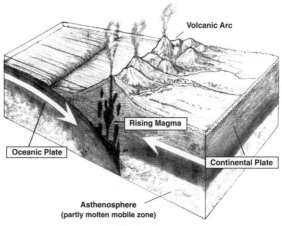

Subduction

Subduction of an oceanic plate and the formation of a volcanic mountain chain, similar to part of the process that gave rise to the formation of the Aspy and Bras d'Or Terranes of Cape Breton Highlands National Park.

downward into the hot interior. This process—called subduction—is usually accompanied by long periods of volcanic activity and earthquakes along the zone of downfolding. As the sinking edge becomes heated, its buoyant material rises toward the surface, elevating the crust and forming a chain of volcanic peaks called an island arc. The rocks of the Bras d'Or Terrane, which underlies the southeast corner of the Park, were once part of an island arc.

About 430 million years ago another volcanic island arc, the Aspy Terrane, emerged close to ancient North America. The roots of this mountain chain also became a piece of the geological jigsaw.

As the continents moved towards each other and the sea continued to shrink, the island chains and their surrounding marine sediments were compressed, metamorphosed and uplifted. Another plate, the Avalon Terrane, after a 40-million-year journey from its origins adjacent to South America, nudged up against the Bras d'Or Terrane, which in turn rear-ended the North American shield. The Aspy Terrane, caught in the crunch between the Blair River Complex and the Bras d'Or Terrane, was forced deep into the earth as the Bras d'Or Terrane rafted over it. As the Aspy Terrane descended, its leading edge melted and rising granite magma from it worked its way into the overlying rocks of the Bras d'Or Terrane, adding to their complexity.

By 350 million years ago, after having been put together and then torn asunder by unimaginable forces, all the continental plates had come together in a supercontinent called Pangea. The four slabs of the Earth's shell that make up Cape Breton Island were assembled in their present arrangement, crushed together in the heart of this supercontinent.

The Rise and Fall of the Acadian Mountains

When continental plates collide, the landscape is reworked for hundreds of kilometres inland from the leading edges, becoming interleaved like shuffled playing cards, or crumpled and folded into high mountain ranges, with granite magma intruding into their cores. The collision between North America and Africa created one such huge mountain belt—the Acadian Mountains—comparable in magnitude to today's Himalayas. And Cape Breton Highlands was a part of the action.

In the middle of Pangea, near the equator, these high mountains were a desert, and because they were devoid of vegetation, erosion was rapid. The sediments were transported to broad basins that developed over what is now the Gulf of St. Lawrence. So much material was deposited in these lowlands that the weight of successive layers caused those parts of the crust to warp and sink. Huge depths of sediments accumulated and spread to cover the entire Maritimes region, where they turned to rock. Today, those rocks are mostly hidden beneath the waters of the Gulf of St. Lawrence, but some of them can be found on the western side of the Park as the coarse sandstones that mantle the slopes of the highlands. Examples are in the roadcut across from the lookoff with the Veterans' monument on French Mountain, and at Presqu'île, at the north end of the ridge between the highway and the ocean.

Age upon age, erosion continued, and the great mountains

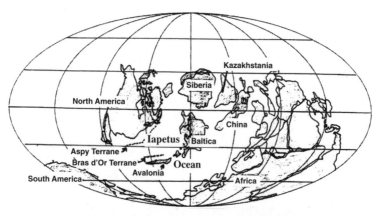

Relative Positions of the Continents about 500 Million Years Ago
The present eastern edge of North America has yet to be added; its pieces are being formed elsewhere as micro-continents. The Aspy and Bras d'Or Terranes, which today make up part of Cape Breton Highlands National Park, are emerging as island arcs in the Iapetus Ocean. Avalonia, part of which will form the Mira Terrane of southeastern Cape Breton, has already completed part of its long northward journey from its origins near South America. The ocean between the spreading plates is not the Atlantic Ocean, but an earlier one called Iapetus, after the father of Atlantis of Greek mythology. The continents will come together and begin spreading again before the Atlantic will be formed.

that rimmed the interior basin were worn down. Eventually, seawater flooded into the basin, forming an inland sea known as the Windsor Sea. Pangea was creeping northward; Cape Breton was approaching the equator and the climate was warming. For some reason, interchange between the inland sea and the distant Tethys Ocean became restricted and sporadic, resulting in repeated flooding and drying of the inland sea. In between puls-

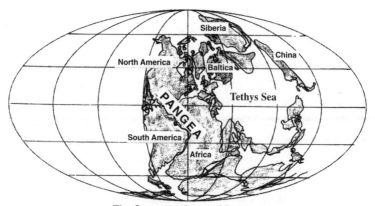

The Supercontinent of Pangea

40

es, the salts within this evaporating body of water became increasingly concentrated and began to precipitate, forming the white gypsum deposits found around the four corners of the Park today—Ingonish, Cape North, Pleasant Bay and Chéticamp.

The Supercontinent Breaks Up

Around 230 million years ago a new phase of continental movement began that resulted in the breakup of Pangea and the opening of the Atlantic Ocean. Now, here's a bit of a twist: the separation did not take place along those faults where the different terranes had originally become joined to North America, but rather to the east, along the outer edge of what is now the continental shelf. Thus, the Maritimes region acquired several exotic chips of the Earth's surface, including former pieces of Africa and South America.

Millimetre by millimetre, the spreading continued. As the continents drifted apart there were renewed cycles of uplift and erosion. After millions of years the land was reduced to almost a flat plain, or peneplain, extending across Nova Scotia into New Brunswick and out onto the continental shelf, with both hard and soft rocks worn down to a more or less common elevation near sea level.

It's mind-boggling how vast mountain ranges the size of the Himalayas could disintegrate into a level plain. But the processes that wore them down are wearing down the Cape Breton Highlands today. It is continually undergoing decomposition. All over the Park, wherever the surface of rock is exposed to the atmosphere, grains of rock decompose and flake off when its minerals swell or shrink as air and water chemically alter them. Water splits rock apart as it freezes and expands in pores or cracks. Lichens secrete acids that dissolve mineral grains in rocks, and plant roots penetrate into cracks in rocks, causing the rock to split.

Gravity pulls down anything from tiny grains to whole mountainsides. On French Mountain long bolts are visible in the cliffs above the roadway where they have been inserted to help anchor the rocks there. The Park's work crews periodically have

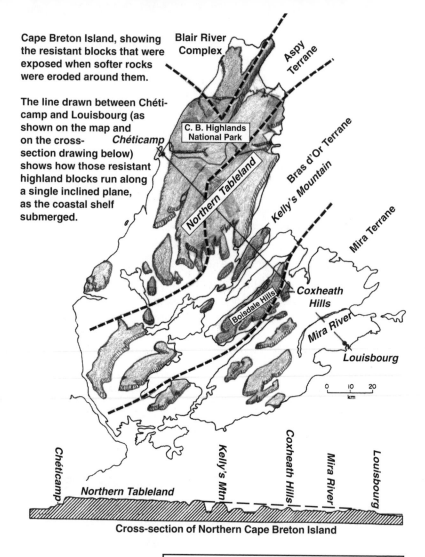

Cape Breton Island, showing the resistant blocks that were exposed when softer rocks were eroded around them.

The line drawn between Chéti-camp and Louisbourg (as shown on the map and on the cross-section drawing below) shows how those resistant highland blocks run along a single inclined plane, as the coastal shelf submerged.

Blair River Complex

Aspy Terrane

C. B. Highlands National Park

Chéticamp

Northern Tableland

Bras d'Or Terrane

Kelly's Mountain

Mira Terrane

Coxheath Hills

Boisdale Hills

Mira River

Louisbourg

0   10   20
km

Chéticamp

Northern Tableland

Kelly's Mtn

Coxheath Hills

Mira River

Louisbourg

Cross-section of Northern Cape Breton Island

As the continents drifted apart after the breakup of Pangea, Cape Breton was near the trailing edge of the North American plate. The area under the trailing margins bulged upward for hundreds of metres as upwelling magma filled the widening rift (A). Erosion rapidly bevelled the elevated landmass to a level plain near sea level. As the bevelled margin moved

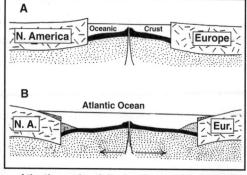

A

N. America   Oceanic   Crust   Europe

B

Atlantic Ocean

N. A.   Eur.

farther away from the influence of the thermal activity, it subsided (B), forming a submerged coastal shelf. The weight of sediments accumulating on the submerged shelf accentuated the tilt.

to dredge the ditches of volumes of loose rock, some chunks the size of washing machines, that fall from the steep slopes. Scree slopes and scars from rock avalanches, common on steep hillsides throughout the Park, can be seen from the hiking trails along the Clyburn and Chéticamp rivers. Mostly, it's a slow process that we rarely notice, but when you consider the almost inconceivably long periods of time involved, and the number of different ways by which erosion occurs, you begin to understand how whole mountain ranges can be reduced to sand and mud.

Rock, soil and trees fall into the ocean wherever the shore is eroded out from under them, or into streams where the banks become undercut. Ocean waves attack the rocky shore by sheer impact, forcing water into joints and cavities under pressure, and creating suction when the waves are suddenly withdrawn. Wave action at the base of the mountainside north of La Bloc is undermining the weak, steeply tilted layers of rock, causing the whole hillside to settle. This slumping has twice required the relocation of the Cabot Trail between La Bloc and Trout Brook. You can see one of the former roadbeds just below the lookoff a kilometre north of La Bloc driveway. Years earlier, a roadway that ran closer to the shore was washed away after the ocean undercut it.

Waves continuously change the shape of the Park's shorelines by piling up sediments on the shore or carrying them away to deeper water. Ocean currents moving along the shore carry sediments eroded from the surrounding hills and shoreline, and deposit these sediments as spits and barrier beaches. The barrier beaches at the mouth of the Chéticamp River and Ingonish Harbour are good examples of this process.

Running water has been the main architect of the landforms of Cape Breton Highlands, eroding and transporting sediments for countless ages. Glaciers, and the waters that issued from them, transported immense quantities of materials across the landscape. The streams that flow from the highlands appear to be undersized for their valleys, but during glacial times they carried much larger volumes of water than they do today. In dry weather the brooks are often not much more than an unimpressive trickle, but their levels can rise dramatically after prolonged rain and in the spring when the winter's accumulation of snow begins to melt. The erosive action of the streams becomes apparent after heavy rains when their sediment loads are dispersed from their mouths in muddy plumes for hundreds of metres out into the ocean.

Ancient Highlands Revealed

Twenty million years ago the Maritime crustal block again became uplifted by several hundred metres, starting another cycle of vigorous erosion. The soft sedimentary rocks were stripped away, exposing the more resistant rocks such as granite that had formed during the earlier period of mountain building, and the buried highlands were exhumed. The old peneplain, which was once at sea level, is today represented by the tops of resistant highland blocks. In the Park, you can get a broad view of the gently rolling top of the plateau from the Cabot Trail by the radio tower, the missile-shaped structure 1.5 km north of French Lake.

As erosion continued, the valleys deepened and lowlands were developed. At times, sea level was lower in relation to the land than it is now, which allowed ancient rivers to cut the exposed surface even deeper than when the land was covered by the sea. The Bras d'Or Lake was deepened to over 250 metres at one point and the exposed Gulf of St. Lawrence became dissected by river valleys that today form deep channels under the waters of the gulf. The beds of gypsum that had formed in the shallow Windsor Sea ages before were uncovered and partially dissolved, forming an irregular topography of sinkholes, pillars and cliffs such as those seen from the Cabot Trail between Cape North Village and the Dingwall turnoff. One of the most prominent landforms in the Park that was formed during this period of differential erosion is the long, straight range of hills known as the Aspy escarpment. You go over that when you climb North Mountain.

Submergence and Flooding

Sometime after the last cycle of uplift and erosion the sea level rose, submerging the coastline. Whether this was due to a worldwide rise in sea level from melting glaciers, subsidence of the land, or a combination of both, is not clear, but the higher sea level inundated coastal bays, river estuaries, the Bras d'Or Lakes, and the channels and basin of the Gulf of St. Lawrence.

Faulting

The stress and strain from all the endless movement produced cracks and joints in the earth's crust. Wherever movement took place along opposite sides of one of these joints, such as along the North Aspy River, a fault was created. We get a look at this fault zone—highly fractured and busted up rock—where the Cabot Trail travels up North Mountain from Big Intervale. The actual fault plane of the escarpment, the so-called Aspy fault, cannot be seen from the road, because it follows the river along the bottom of the valley. But by following the river on foot, you can see where it is exposed occasionally in the river bed, with the different types of rocks on either side of the fault plane.

Rocks along fault zones are affected in different ways. Where pressures are low, the rocks are broken up and ground to powder. Where pressures are higher, the temperatures due to friction are sufficient to weld the rocks back together again. Along the steep side of MacGregor Brook ravine, near the top of North Mountain, the road cut exposes broken sedimentary and volcanic rocks that have been highly altered by heat and pressure. Narrow dykes of pink granite cut older rocks, and in some places are so inextricably intermingled with the older rocks that a composite rock results. Near the top of the ascent you can even see actual surfaces of movement—the places where one part of the rock moved past another. Here the rocks are so thoroughly broken and sheared by faulting it would be difficult to obtain a solid piece more than 15 cm long.

Another example of a fault can be seen in the road cut near the top of the hill 400 metres south of Corney Brook campground entrance. Here the contact is very distinct between the pink granite on the north and the dark gray schist on the south.

Faults control the course of most of the Park's rivers, which tend to take advantage of the planes of weakness created by the

Formation of the Aspy Escarpment

A. Parts of the old Acadian Mountains were overlain by sediments.

B. Massive faulting brought the weaker sediments opposite more resistant rock.

C. Erosion reduced the whole region to a common level. The region was then uplifted, permitting another cycle of erosion.

D. Weaker rocks were removed from the south side of the fault line.

E. Partial submergence of the region led to flooding of the lowlands around Aspy Bay.

Different views of this dramatic landscape can be seen while driving along the Cabot Trail between North Mountain and South Mountain.

fractured rock.

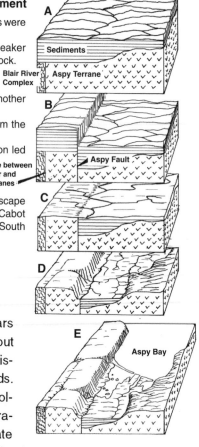

The Legacy of the Ice Age

Two or three million years ago the latest chapter was about to be written in the geological history of the Cape Breton Highlands. The earth's climate became cooler, and average world temperatures suddenly started to fluctuate in cycles that lasted for hundreds of centuries. In periods of declining temperatures rain would fall as snow. As each winter became a little colder the snow built up a little deeper and stayed a little longer until one year it was too deep for the summer sun to melt away. As the winters got colder the snow continued to accumulate, eventually becoming compacted and re-crystallized into ice. Finally, there was only the deep chill of endless winter.

When ice reaches a thickness of 60 metres or more it will flow outward due to the pressure of its own weight, moving at rates from a few centimetres to tens of metres a day depending on the retarding effects of the contact surface at its sides and base. In the last 1.5 million years eastern Canada has undergone several major cycles of glacial advance and retreat, with the ice sheet sometimes extending well out onto the continental shelf. The latest one began around 75 thousand years ago. A warming trend began about 18,000 years ago and since then the glaciers, with temporary halts, have been gradually receding.

Although these glaciations subjected portions of the Highlands to extensive erosion, the major features of the Park's landscape—the hills, valleys and coastline shaped during the previous hundreds of millions of years—remained intact. The valleys were deepened and widened but are not substantially different from their pre-ice age courses.

The lowlands, on the other hand, have been considerably modified after being buried with glacial deposits. The ice sheet bulldozed the surface soil, often down to the underlying bedrock where it plucked out stones and boulders, engulfed them within the mass of ice, carried them for some distance and dropped them again when the ice melted. Drainage patterns were disrupted, streams were blocked and redirected, and many lakes, ponds and bogs were formed. The Chéticamp River found its present outlet blocked for a time by a glacier in the Gulf of St. Lawrence, and the river's course was diverted to flow temporarily through the Rigwash Valley. Meltwater streams inside the glacier transported and distributed huge quantities of till, the general name given to material scraped from the bedrock and deposited under or in front of glaciers.

Some of the glacial deposits in the Park are over 50 m thick. In the lower reaches of Clyburn Brook, the stream's bedrock channel lies 50 to 100 metres below the load of boulders that you see from the trail. As much as two thirds of the water that comes down the river actually flows unseen underneath the boulders. You can see cross sections of till deposits especially along the shore wherever the eroding sand and gravel banks overlie the bedrock. Trout Brook and Broad Cove are two such places. The stone fences and mounds of rock that are still sometimes seen in woods that were once old fields are testimony to the labour of those who tried to cultivate the region's stony soil.

Glaciers that flowed from the plateau occupied most of the major valleys in the Park. Glaciated valleys have a characteristic

U-shape, as opposed to the more V-shaped profile of unglaciated valleys. This U shape can be seen in the Chéticamp, Grande Anse, North Aspy and Clyburn valleys. The valleys of Fishing Cove Brook and MacGregor Brook retain the more V-shaped profile of unglaciated valleys.

Tributary valleys contained smaller glaciers which, because of their smaller size, failed to deepen the tributary valley at the same rate as the main glacier deepened the main valley. The truncated ends of these side valleys were left "hanging" above the floor of the main valley when the glaciers retreated. Beulach Ban Brook and Little Southwest Brook, tributaries of the North Aspy River, are examples of hanging valleys, which can be seen from the lookoffs on North Mountain. As you stand on these lookoffs on a hot day in July it's hard to envision a river of ice moving down this valley, a creeping tongue of the great ice sheet that entombed the land.

Changing Sea Levels

Sea level has continued to rise since the last retreat of the glaciers. The relative rise in sea level may be due to the increasing volume of water in the ocean from melting ice, or to crustal subsidence, or to a combination of both. Whatever the reason, sea level in Cape Breton is rising by at least 30 cm per century, and there is evidence that the western side of the island may be sinking at more than twice that rate. Eventually Cape Breton might be divided into a number of islands as the low-lying passages between the highlands become filled by the sea.

Although virtually the entire region was covered by ice during the last glaciation, certain areas of the plateau, including North Mountain, lack any trace of its passage. It may be that the base of the ice sheet was frozen to the ground because the ice was thinner on the highlands, or some areas may have actually projected through the ice sheet as nunataks, and thus may have escaped glaciation.

The last ice cap disappeared from Cape Breton about 9,000 years ago in the area now occupied by the Chéticamp reservoir.

4

Animal Life

As WITH THE PROVINCE'S FLORA, successive glaciations completely obliterated animal life from that area of Nova Scotia now above sea level. As the climate warmed, land animals followed the retreating ice, and freshwater species moved from one river to another along the coast through the water supplied by the melting ice. It is possible that Ice Age animals were able to live on parts of the then-exposed outer limits of the continental shelf and that the first occupants of what is now Cape Breton Highlands migrated from land that is now far beneath the sea. Large numbers of mastodon and mammoth teeth and bones—even dung-balls—have been recovered by fishermen dragging these offshore banks.

Because of the barrier presented by the Strait of Canso, not every species that eventually colonized mainland Nova Scotia got as far as Cape Breton Island. Since the completion of the Canso Causeway in 1955, a solid ice bridge forms between Cape Breton and the mainland, which encourages the movement of larger mammals such as bobcat and coyote.There are still no woodchucks. Only recently have a porcupine and skunk been reported on the island, but there may not yet be a breeding population here. No races of animals have developed that are peculiar to the island itself, but compared with other islands in the Gulf of St. Lawrence, Cape Breton Island is relatively rich in mammals.

Compared to the rest of Nova Scotia, a relatively low number of reptile and amphibian species inhabit the Park. Typical of the species you are likely to see in the Park are the Maritime garter snake, leopard frog and green frog, and red-back and yellow-spotted salamanders. This dearth is likely due to colder temperatures here, a more limited habitat, and the barrier presented by the Strait of Canso. None of our snakes are poisonous.

Cape Breton Highlands is one of the best places anywhere to see moose in the wild. The first sight of a mature bull moose leaves you in awe. Their sheer size, if not their extraordinary design, is impressive. These imposing animals can weigh up to 600 kilograms. I remember watching one from the side of the road one day, along with a visitor who was so excited he left his car in the middle of the highway with the doors open and ran up to where I was standing. "I've hunted moose from Maine to Alaska," he exclaimed, "but I've never seen one the size of that in my life!" With his huge bulk and full rack of antlers—the moose, I mean—he was certainly an impressive sight.

Moose live mainly on the plateau, but you see them in the lowlands too. The hiking trails where you are most likely to see them are the Skyline, Bog, and Benjies Lake trails on the western side of the Park, and Glasgow Lakes, Branch Pond Lookoff and Franey trails on the eastern side.

It's been said that a moose looks like a horse designed by a committee. In spite of their ungainly appearance they are superbly adapted to life in the Park's forests. Even the tiny calves, at the age of only a few days, can outrun a human and swim readily. The lordly bulls grow a new set of antlers every summer and shed them in autumn or early winter. During the period of growth the antlers are soft and spongy, with blood vessels running through them, covered by a soft, skin-like casing that looks like velvet. The antlers harden in late summer and the velvet is rubbed off against tree trunks.

During the mating season, or rut, in late September, the bulls use their antlers to spar against one another for the right to breed with one or more cows. I watched a couple of them in a shoving match one day along the edge of a lake. They lowered their heads, locked antlers and pushed each other around until the larger of the two shoved the other one over the bank backwards into the lake. The cold water didn't diminish his ardour, however, for he climbed back out, caught up with his rival and they both tagged along behind a couple of females, pausing every little while to engage in another round of shoving. They don't seem to inflict any serious damage, but park warden Randy Thompson told me he once saw two moose that had their antlers inextricably locked. I've often wondered what it feels like for moose to carry these heavy racks, but it must be even more cumbersome when the antler on one side is shed before the other.

The fellow who stopped to see the moose had gone back to his car to get a camera. The next thing I knew he was across the ditch, stumbling toward the moose with the camera up to his face, guided by the little image in his viewfinder, and popping off flashes as he went. Now, moose are generally pretty docile if you leave them alone; it's really unusual to hear of them coming after anyone, even people who go on vacation and leave their brains at home. Luckily, this moose bolted for the nearby woods, moving with a grace and swiftness that belied its awkward appearance. It stopped for a moment at the edge of the barren, then with a few steps melded into the forest with hardly a sound.

Moose were plentiful at the time of European settlement of Cape Breton in the 1700s, and became an integral part of the trade and economy of the times. Large herds of moose and caribou in the northern parts of the island afforded sustenance to the settlers and aboriginals. Thousands were killed by New England colonists primarily for the hides, which were exported, and the noses, which were considered a delicacy. It is said that nearly 9,000 were killed in one winter alone, and the stench from their decaying carcasses was perceived by the crews of vessels passing along the northeastern coast of the highlands. By 1800 they were virtually wiped out in Cape Breton, and for the next 150 years they remained rare. In 1947-48, eighteen moose were captured at Elk Island National Park in Alberta and released at Roper's Brook on the eastern side of Cape Breton Highlands. Today they number in the thousands on the island's northern peninsula, and since the 1970s there has been an annual hunt outside the Park.

Foxes are common throughout the Park. I often see them loping along the Cabot Trail in their attractive coat of lustrous red fur and large bushy tail. Although their basic colour is reddish, their natural hair colour, like that of humans, can vary from blond to black. This variation in colour may be due in part to the mating of wild foxes with ranch-raised foxes that were bred for certain colours and released in times of declining fur prices.

One evening on North Mountain I was sitting at the edge of the bank overlooking the ravine on the Grande Anse side of the mountain. There are no lookoffs on that side of the mountain, unfortunately, and the shoulder of the road is not wide enough to park on. But you can walk, stopping to enjoy the view whenever you want. As you walk further up the road from the Lone Shieling, you can look down with a bird's-eye view onto the forest of sugar maples cradled in the valley below. The valley beside you narrows into a ravine as you ascend the hill, and the steep slopes across the chasm side draw closer and closer. At a bluff overlooking the ravine I stepped over the guardrail and sat down with my back against one of its posts. The valley was still—just a murmur from the stream hidden in the bottom of the ravine and a couple of thrushes singing from somewhere in the hills. To the west the valley stretched away towards the village of Pleasant Bay. The smell of the sea wafted up the valley and a low bank of fog moved in from the gulf to blanket the village. The sun was painting the hillsides in subtle shades of mauve and other colours I don't even know if there are names for.

After I'd sat there a while I noticed a fox coming up the road. He appeared to be hunting, occasionally weaving in and out among the guardrail posts to check the grass for something or other. I just sat there, watching. He didn't seem to be in any hurry; who would be on such an evening? I was on the ravine side of the guardrail when he finally came abreast of me on the pavement. He trotted by me a few paces and, getting my scent, stopped as if he had run into an invisible wall. He turned, saw me, stood there for a moment, then sat down at the edge of the pavement, watching me with eyes half closed. He yawned. I yawned. I thought he was going to fall asleep. After a while he got up, slipped under the railing, stepped to the edge of the ravine as if admiring the view, and nonchalantly sat down an arm's length away. For about five minutes we both sat there, gazing out over the ravine, sharing the quiet scene surrounding us. Then he casually got up, stretched, went back under the railing and kept going up the road.

Foxes have a reputation for pilfering. One item they seem to covet is golf balls, and they have been known to complicate a golfer's score-keeping by dashing onto a green and disappearing with his ball. One day some people showed up at a Park Visitor Centre inquiring where the fox den was located at the MacIntosh Brook campground. Since the Park doesn't keep a registry of fox dwellings, the staff weren't able to help him. Still, the visitors persisted. The attendant wondered why they wanted to know the whereabouts of the den. Pointing to his stockinged feet, one of the visitors replied, "Because he's got our shoes!" The unsuspecting campers had left their shoes on a picnic table overnight and a fox had run off with them.

Coyotes are a fairly recent addition to the Park's wildlife, arriving here in the late 1970s. They are one of the few mammals that have succeeded in extending its territory despite the spread of civilization. Their range expansion from western North America in the last 100 years is unparalleled by any other mammal in recent history. They adapt to various habitats and can survive on anything from grass and grasshoppers to deer mice and deer.

There are many theories about the origins of the eastern coyote, which is much larger—closer to a wolf in size—than its western cousin. Although coyotes may breed with dogs, the resulting hybrid has a delayed breeding season that results in the pups being born in midwinter, which makes survival and the establishment of a viable population of "coydogs" unlikely. There is some speculation that the eastern coyote is indigenous to eastern North America. What used to be called the brush wolf by the early settlers, to distinguish it from the larger timber wolf, may in fact have been the eastern coyote, and possibly these animals were always there, surviving in small populations in the eastern states and Canada. But most scientific evidence points to an ad-

Animal Tracks and Scat

Bear: 9-15 cm

Front paw

Both the front and hind paws have a heel pad, but it's more developed on the hind.

Hind paw

Ruffed Grouse: 50-70 mm, toe to heel

Weasel and Mink: 25-90 cm

Bobcat: 50-70 mm; **Lynx**: 75-85 mm (greater if you include thick fur surrounding the pads)

The size and appearance of tracks vary with depth and firmness of snow, and you will not see such detail in snow.

Red Fox: 40-60 mm
Coyote: 45-70 mm

Snowshow Hare

up to 18 cm

Weasel: 25-55 mm
Mink: 55-85 mm

Photographs by Clarence Barrett

ABOVE: **Chéticamp River canyon.**
BELOW: **L'Acadien Trail above Chéticamp River estuary and Petit Étang beach.**
RIGHT: **Moose on French Mountain.**

OPPOSITE PAGE. TOP: **Black Point, Ingonish; Cape Smokey in background.**
CENTRE LEFT: **Skyline Trail in winter.** CENTRE RIGHT: **Shoreline south of Trout Brook.** BOTTOM: **Snowy taiga, interior plateau.**

THIS PAGE. TOP: **Squeaker Hole near Black Brook, Coastal and Jack Pine Trails.** BOTTOM: **Sunset, Gulf of St. Lawrence.**

TOP LEFT: **Kelp (seaweed) at ocean's edge.** TOP RIGHT: **Backcountry skiing, eastern highlands; Money Point in background.** ABOVE: **Ocean at Black Brook.** RIGHT: **Sundew, Bog Trail.** BELOW LEFT: **Schist cliffs, north of Trout Brook.** BELOW RIGHT: **South of Corney Brook; Presqu'île and Chéticamp Island in background.**

TOP LEFT: **Along Coastal Trail.** TOP RIGHT: **From Mount Franey, looking east over Clyburn Valley and Cape Smokey.** ABOVE LEFT: **Hemlocks, Clyburn Valley.** RIGHT: **Blueberry bushes in the autumn, Glasgow Lakes Trail.** BELOW: **Sea caves below French Mountain.**

TOP: Rigwash Valley from La Grande Falaise, north of Chéticamp. CENTRE LEFT: Taiga, central plateau, looking toward Aspy escarpment. CENTRE RIGHT: Trail at Middle Head. BOTTOM: Sugar maples in fall near the Lone Shieling.

TOP LEFT: Looking south from French Mountain; Chéticamp Island in background. TOP RIGHT: Tamarack, sedges, and blueberry bushes on heath barrens, Glasgow Lakes Trail. CENTRE: L'Acadien Trail. BOTTOM: Highland plateau; MacKenzie River valley in foreground.

TOP: **From Mount Franey, looking west up Clyburn Valley.** CENTRE LEFT: **Le Buttereau and Chéticamp River estuary.** CENTRE RIGHT: **Aspy River tributary.** BOTTOM: **Backcountry camping near Lone Lake, eastern highlands.**

Moose scat, winter

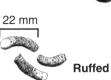

Snowshoe Hare

10 mm

22 mm

Ruffed Grouse

Moose scat, summer

Bobcat or **Lynx**

In winter, moose browse mostly on dry woody food that results in pellets. In summer, when more herbaceous plants are available, their scat may be more of a plop.

Lynx scat contains a lot of rodent and snowshoe hare hair. It tends to be more segmented than coyote scat and lacks the large bones often found there. Its diameter is 15-19 mm.

Fox or **Coyote**

Coyote and fox scat may look similar. Winter scat contains mostly hair; summer scat contains berries. If it has large pieces of bone or is more than 19 mm diameter, it is probably coyote. Less than 16 mm, fox.

Mink: 55-85 mm

Red Squirrel: 9-12 mm

Moose:
9-15 cm wide

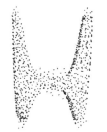

Red squirrel track and, below, as it looks in soft snow

mixture of wolf genes in the eastern coyote, acquired as their ancestors began to extend their range from the prairies of mid-western North America.

Coyotes usually shun wolves, with good reason, as wolves generally won't tolerate them. However, as coyotes moved farther from their traditional range, individuals on the leading edge of the expansion would often be solitary animals wandering far from the company of others of their species. In such circumstances, without the presence of their own kind to associate with, it sometimes occurred that relationships would be consummated between coyotes and wolves.

The wolves are gone now from Atlantic Canada, extirpated by the mid-1800s, but its forests, including those here in the Park, echo with the cries and barks of their hybrid descendants. The boisterous yips, howling, baying and yodeling of coyotes when they get together can be a hair-raising experience. Two coyotes howling in unison can create the illusion of several performing in concert. If there are several in the vicinity, the howling of one triggers the others. One night I was camped on a barren knoll and had gotten out a tin whistle to while away some time before I turned in. I no sooner had started to play than I found myself accompanied by an invisible but clamorous audience. Either my playing was bad, or they were just being sociable, but they set up such a din that they must have wakened every forest creature for miles around.

Both foxes and coyotes are sometimes seen begging for handouts, especially at roadside lookoffs where they strike charming poses beside the large signs that strictly forbid the feeding of wildlife. Giving in to the temptation to feed such animals inevitably leads to problems for both animals and humans. For humans it sometimes means getting bitten as the animals become more aggressive in their demands to be fed. For the animals themselves it often means death; they have to be destroyed when they bite, or they are struck by cars as they become less wary of traffic.

In some years snowshoe hares, or "rabbits" as they are commonly called, seem to be everywhere in Cape Breton Highlands. I remember, in years of abundance, that driving along the highway produced a wave, like falling dominos, as the hares jumped back from the edge of the road upon my approach.

Like many animals, hares exhibit wide cyclic fluctuations in their numbers. They are very prolific and have the potential to increase rapidly to a peak, after which a rapid and often dramatic decline sets in. During the winter of 1998-99 it was almost impossible to put your foot down in the Park without stepping on a hare track. Two years later they were as scarce as flamingos. I skied for months that winter without seeing a single track, and benevolent societies in the area had to cancel their annual rabbit suppers due to the scarcity. The decline seems to be due to a combination of predation and the starvation and disease that results from overcrowding of its habitat as the population reaches a peak.

Like some other animals—moose, for example—hares digest their food more than once. But not in the same manner as moose. Moose devour large quantities of forage, which they hastily chew and temporarily store in a large chamber called a rumen. From here the food passes into a second chamber that contains numerous small compartments that pack the food into small masses called cuds. These cuds are regurgitated when the animal is resting and the vegetation is thoroughly chewed. It is then swallowed a second time and passed through the rest of the digestive system. If you think that's gross, wait till you hear this. Some of the food that goes into the stomach of hares is defecated as a soft, partly-digested, jelly-like pellet. The hare then eats these "green pellets," digests them, and poops again. The recycled pellets are the harder pellets we see on the ground.

Black bears are occasionally sighted along the Rigwash Valley in early summer where they turn over boulders and logs searching for ants and grubs. Later on, when the blueberries ripen, they sometimes graze on the steep, open hillsides above the lookoff at Cap Rouge and across from the lookoffs at Jumping Brook. I've also seen them in the Clyburn and Grande Anse valleys where they feed on apples from trees that were once part of old farms, and on open blueberry barrens in the interior of the Park. You sometimes see bear scat on trails, usually in the form of a blackish mound containing evidence of their last meal: ant skeletons, blueberries, the orange berries of mountain ash.

After reading some of the literature on traveling in bear country you may never want to set foot in the woods again. But bears are one of our shyest animals and they use their well-developed senses of sight, hearing and smell to avoid humans. Bears will usually leave if they are aware of your presence, and so far as I know there has never been a bear attack in Cape Breton Highlands National Park—or, for that matter, all of Cape Breton. Still, they are wild animals and they deserve respect. I've seen people get out of their cars and walk across the road to photograph bear cubs while the mother bear, unbeknownst to them, was grazing in the ditch behind their back bumper. Perhaps only one bear in a hundred would mean any harm in such a situation, but, unfortunately, they don't come in numerical order. In the rare event that you do encounter a bear remain calm, leave the animal an escape route, and back off slowly—don't run.

Bears appear awkward as they shuffle along, but can move with amazing speed if necessary. For short distances they have been clocked at speeds up to 50 kph. They're also good swimmers and climbers. So forget about climbing a tree; all that will do is give you a better view of the scenery while the bear climbs up after you.

Bears are not fussy about what they eat. They'll chow down on just about anything that's available—nuts, berries, insects. Dead meat and garbage is considered a delicacy, and the more decomposed the better. Reminds me of our dog. One night I left some garbage in a can outside the warden station where I was living. Next morning I was awakened to the sound of a flock of excited crows who were happily picking away at an assortment of food scraps that had been strewn across the yard by a bear. I never used the garbage can after that, but every few weeks, ever hopeful, the bear would come by and roll it down the hill towards the woods.

Winter Wildlife

A walk in the winter woods reveals a surprising amount of wildlife activity. I find tracks whenever I'm on skis or snowshoes. When the snow is frozen, it may even be possible to walk on it without sinking, but there has to be at least a dusting of powder on top to capture footprints. You can follow a hiking trail or even walk along the shoulder of the Cabot Trail to see tracks, but you will probably find more tracks if you follow your nose through the woods. Even if you don't use a compass you should be able to find your way out by retracing your own tracks in the snow. A field guide to animal tracks is helpful in their identification.

I nearly always see the tracks of red squirrels whenever I go in the woods. In firm snow their tracks resemble a smaller version of a hare's track, but in softer snow they look more like the H-shaped Honda logo. You will likely find squirrel tracks and not those of chipmunks because chipmunks hibernate during winter. Often the tracks lead to the base of a tree or disappear into a hole in the snow that leads to a tunnel. Tunnels can be quite extensive, leading from tree to tree, or to food stashes made by the squirrel.

Another sure sign of a squirrel is a midden—a pile of cone scales that accumulates over the years below some trees in a coniferous forest. Squirrels like to take the cones to a favourite eating spot—a tree stump or branch—and perch there, stripping the cones of their scales and extracting their seeds. Squirrels also nip off the tips of conifer twigs, especially spruces, to get at the twigs' terminal buds, and I often see parts of the ground littered with these twigs.

You might come across the paired prints of a short-tailed weasel, or ermine, leading to a small heap of blood-stained fur—the remnants of a vole, perhaps. This efficient little predator kills animals up to five times its size, including muskrats, waterfowl, squirrels and hares.

The weasel's generic name, Mustela, means "one who carries off mice." Although their tracks can be numerous, the animals themselves are hard to spot in winter, because they are snowy white except for a black tip on their tail. They turn mostly dark brown in the spring.

Like the weasel, the mink most commonly leaves a pattern of paired footprints, but patterns also include prints in groups of three and four. The paired footprint pattern is created because the hind feet drop into the hole made by the front paws—so, both front and hind paws touch the same place as he runs. The word mink comes from the Swedish word menk, which means "the stinking animal from Finland." Like other members of the weasel family, the mink has an anal musk gland that discharges a liquid as malodorous as that of a skunk. Fortunately, it does not spray like a skunk, and its scent does not carry very far. Tracking mink requires a lot of energy. I've followed their trails through thickets of trees and underbrush, across bogs and marshes, and through icy streams. Often its tracks disappear under the snow and emerge several metres further along.

Shrews leave a zipper-like track about as wide as an adult person's thumb. If you follow the trail you will probably see it disappear down an entryway to a world beneath the snow.

One of the most unusual and puzzling trails to come across consists of a wide, shallow trough through the snow—the trail of an otter. When otters move on the snow, they tend to bound a few steps, then get down on their belly and slide, pushing themselves along with their short legs, creating a trough from 15 to 25cm wide. This is not the only kind of trail they leave, but their other track patterns can often be identified by a conspicuous tail drag in the snow.

When snowshoe hares are abundant the number of their footprints only a few hours after a fresh snowfall is amazing. The shape of the elongated "snowshoe" print left by each hind foot is a clue to which way a hare is going. The widest part, the toe end, points in the hare's direction of travel, the same as a snowshoe does. When a hare runs or hops, its smaller front feet land first, then the larger hind feet are brought forward to pass to the outside and around the front feet to land in front of them. The urine of snowshoe hares sometimes appears as a faint yellow to reddish stain on the snow (I've seen it), and smells faintly of pine (so

I'm told). The hare's colour varies from brown in summer to white in winter, but it is not the presence or absence of snow, nor high or low temperatures, that causes the hare to shed its fur and grow another colour. Rather, the change is a response to the changing amount of daylight in the spring and fall.

The Canada lynx and the bobcat are common but rarely seen recluses in Cape Breton Highlands. Their solitary tracks in the snow more often betray their presence than does an actual sighting. You are just as likely to see a lynx or bobcat along the Cabot Trail as on any particular path. The two cats are very similar in appearance, and often difficult to tell apart. The most certain distinguishing feature, if you can get a look at it, is the tail. The tip of the bobcat's tail is black only on the top, while the entire tip of the lynx tail is black. Also, the black tufts of the lynx's ear tips are more prominent than the bobcat's. Both animals travel much more at night than in daytime, which make them even harder to see, but even if you don't get to see one it's fun to look for their tracks.

I came up behind a lynx one time along an old abandoned road up on the plateau. The lynx had his back to me and was slowly stepping along the grassy trail about thirty metres ahead, completely unaware of my presence. I followed behind it for a little ways, step for step, as quietly as I could. But the lynx must have gotten a whiff of me, for it stopped and whipped its head around, peered at me for several seconds, then bounded up the steep bank beside the trail into the trees. I kept walking, but as I approached the place in the trail where the lynx had disappeared, I half hesitated to continue. The limbs of the trees at that spot were hanging right out over the trail, and I had visions of ten kilograms of wildcat dropping from the branches and sinking its claws into me. In spite of knowing very well that lynx don't attack people, a little twinge of fear went through me as I approached the arching branches.

Then, when I passed directly under the spot, without warning there was an explosion at my feet as a ruffed grouse burst from its cover and flew off through the trees. I managed to keep control of most of my bodily functions except for my heartbeat, but I think that if I had gotten my hands on that bird then and there, I would have done it egregious harm. If you have ever had your heart stopped by the sudden lift-off from the bushes at your feet of a feathered football with wings, you'll understand. Every time a ruffed grouse gets me like that I think, "You stupid bird, if you had just stayed where you were I would never have known you were there. Was all that commotion really necessary?" After my pulse stops racing I must admit that if the element of surprise has the same effect on the bird's predators as it does on the rest of us—that of stunned inertia—it's a pretty useful escape strategy.

As far as feline predators go, lynx had the island to themselves until construction of the causeway between Cape Breton Island and the Nova Scotia mainland allowed the immigration of their close cousin, the bobcat. Because the two cats are so similar in their habitat requirements and in the way they make their livelihoods, biologists say that they occupy the same niche in nature. But there is a principle of ecology that two species cannot live together indefinitely in the same niche. That is, species that are identical in the food they eat and the habitat they use will inevitably be in such direct competition with each other that one of them will have to go, or be eliminated. One species will always have some trait that gives it an edge, however slight, over the other. The bobcat, for example, has by nature a more belligerent disposition than the milder-mannered lynx. Consequently, the lynx, in avoiding the combative behaviour of the bobcat, has in effect been forced to retreat to the hills. The lynx, however, has larger feet than the bobcat. This allows it to travel in the deeper snow of its highland domain, where the bobcat is unable to cope. Cape Breton Highlands has thus become one of the last refuges in the Maritimes for the Canada lynx.

The lynx is a highly specialized predator, particularly adapted for capturing snowshoe hares, its primary prey. Its front end is equipped with sharp fangs and inch-long claws. Its rear end reminds me of a dragster, with its high, powerful hind legs capable of explosive bursts of speed over short distances. This specialization has its drawbacks, though. The lynx is not big enough to capture larger prey such as moose, yet it's not small enough to get by on smaller prey such as mice. Researchers in Cape Breton Highlands found that lynx preyed almost exclusively on snowshoe hare in winter. Its dependence on a single prey is so great that in years when hares are scarce there is a corresponding decline in the numbers of lynx.

After the crash of the hare population in 1989, lynx were hard pressed to find alternative prey. People began to report stories of lynx hanging around rural communities, accepting handouts from humans. I watched one specimen of skin and grief one day walking dejectedly along the ditch beside the Cabot Trail on MacKenzie Mountain. It was quite indifferent to my presence, or to the passing traffic, and I followed it for several hundred metres. At one point it became attracted by a squirrel that was scuffling around in the leaves just inside the woods. Slowly, silently, the lynx paced toward this morsel, lifting one paw, waiting patiently, carefully placing the paw down, lifting the other paw, standing motionless, poised to spring if the squirrel got close enough.

But the squirrel moved out of range and ended up in the trees. Seeing that it was no use, the lynx made his way back to the ditch, with the spiteful little squirrel hurling insults after him from the branches. The lynx appeared to be fed up, perhaps thinking, "Oh the ignominy of it all; reduced to catching squirrels."

I've occasionally seen bear tracks in the winter. Around the first snowfall, a bear finds a place to den in a dense thicket or under a windfall, or in a hollow in a hillside, just large enough to accommodate it when it's curled up. However a denning bear is not truly hibernating, since its body temperature remains normal and its rate of metabolism is only slightly reduced. I read that most bears can be aroused if prodded sufficiently (although I'm not sure why anyone would want to do that), and if the weather is not too cold some bears may wake up and wander around for short periods.

One day while skiing I saw a bear bounding away from me

down a hard-packed slope. I wanted so badly to get a picture that I continued skiing down the hill behind him, fumbling with my pack trying to get the camera out and letting drop my ski poles which were getting in the way. Bad move. I quickly lost my balance on an icy section, tried unsuccessfully to turn without the poles, slid into a tree stump that was poking through the snow, and snapped my ski tip. Oh how I wished I was carrying a spare tip. The trip in that day had been mostly uphill and I was looking forward to an easy, downhill ride out before dark. Now, you'd think, in theory, that it would be possible to glide along on one ski, propelling yourself like you would on a scooter. It worked after a fashion where the snow was firm, but in the soft snow, which was most of the way, my ski-less foot just punched a hole in the snow and sank. I had many miles to go that night before I reached the town-o, hobbling along on the one good ski, and the broken one lashed to my other foot to serve as a snowshoe.

Bear cubs are born in January or February while the mother is sleeping in her winter den, and they nurse there until spring. There are usually two of them and they each weigh about 280 grams (10 ounces), the highest weight ratio among mammals of a mother to her newborn.

You frequently come across the in-line tracks of a ruffed grouse, with one foot carefully placed ahead of the other as if the bird had been walking a tightrope.

While most of the Park's bird species head south for the winter, some stay. Perhaps the most commonly seen bird during the winter months is the black-capped chicadee. They roam the woods in groups hunting for insect eggs and seeds, investigating every nook, prying under bark, into cracks and under the eaves of Park buildings. They seem to hang upside down as much as they perch right-side up. The little birds have quite a fight during the winter against starvation and stinging cold. Ornithologists suspect that chickadees conserve body fat reserves during winter nights by allowing their body temperatures to drop nearly 15 degrees below their daytime temperature, thus slowing down their metabolism. Like other birds, they also tense tiny muscles in their skin that raise feathers and trap an insulating layer of air, much like a down jacket. And they develop extra fluff in their winter plumage by growing 25 to 30 percent more feathers than in summer.

Chickadees can shiver, too, in order to generate heat. During shivering, antagonistic muscles contract simultaneously, which means no external work is done and all the energy produced appears as heat inside the body.

Sometimes the silence of the winter woods is broken by the crackling chatter of white-winged crossbills. The bird is named in part for its peculiar bill with its overlapping tips, and in part for—well, you can probably guess. This arrangement seems clumsy for foraging, but crossbills eat mostly spruce seeds, and their bills are perfectly designed to pry open the seed cones. When a crossbill closes its bill, the bill tips separate the overlapping scales, which allows the bird to seize the seed with its tongue. A flock of them foraging in a spruce canopy can actually create a shower of cone scales.

Most bird species mate only in spring and early summer, but the white-winged crossbill has two distinct breeding seasons: early January to late April and early July to late September. Like moose, white-winged crossbills will lick salt from the winter roads.

The gray jay is another winter resident, maintaining a territory year-round instead of migrating in order to nest. The sudden appearance of this charming, inquisitive jay is a welcome sight in the spruce and fir forests of Cape Breton Highlands. Its flight is soft and soundless—a contrast with its voice, which consists of a variety of chatter, chuckles, whistles and the mimicking of other birds. Gray jays mate for life, and defend a small home territory of about half a square kilometre. To survive on such a small area these birds have developed a technique for storing food against lean times. First they roll the food in their throat until it becomes coated with sticky saliva, then they hide it in a knothole or some crevice in the bark of a tree, where it keeps until needed, even for years.

Other signs of wildlife in the woods in winter are twigs and bark browsed by moose, deer and hares; and scrape marks left on tree bark by moose and deer. You can even smell some animals before you see them. Sometimes when skiing in the woods I come to places where the deep snow has been trampled down by moose, a sort of bedroom and pantry area where the moose can browse and rest. The numerous tracks, along with a rather nice barnyard smell, are an indication that one or more moose are not very far away, perhaps even watching me through the trees.

Reporting Wildlife Sightings

The animals of the Park vary in their abundance, and in their frequency of sighting. Even relatively abundant animals may not be seen often if they are on the go mostly at night, or are secretive in their habits. The Park Warden Service is interested in hearing reports of the rare and uncommon animals in the Park, and they will gladly provide you with wildlife sighting cards if you'd like to record your observations. The form asks you to note, if you can, the animal's age, sex, behaviour, and when and where you saw it. Some animals are so common, of course, that there is really no point in reporting them: moose, fox, hare and squirrel, for example. But even those species, if you find them dead without any apparent cause, should be reported. Park wardens usually send such animals, or tissue samples from them, to the Canadian Cooperative Wildlife Health Centre in Prince Edward Island. Necropsies done on the carcasses can provide information on the health of animal populations and about diseases that may be affecting them.

We all bring home with us stories and memories of meeting wildlife from our visits to Cape Breton Highlands National Park. That's not to say that on every day or every outing some dramatic encounter will occur; sometimes they may be no more than fleeting glimpses. It can be rewarding just to come across the track of a wild animal in the snow or a tuft of moose hair on a branch, and knowing that somewhere nearby a wild creature is sharing your world.

5

Hiking and Ski Trails

THERE ARE 25 OFFICIAL TRAILS in Cape Breton Highlands National Park. This chapter gives a description of each trail, its length and steepness, as well as notes on features that might be overlooked. Of course, what might be a ho-hum trail on one day can turn out to be just the place for a satisfying excursion on another, simply because of a change in the weather or because of some little incident: the smell of salt rime drying on the rocks, or the sudden fragrance of hay-scented fern on a mountain trail; the pattern on the tail feather of a ruffed grouse; the look on your three-year-old's face when a squirrel jumps upon a rock and performs its fidgety little dance before her. Little kids aren't particularly struck on grand scenery, but let them find a hollow tree trunk to crawl inside, a pile of dried moose poop to fling at each other, or a brook or puddle, and you'd best have along a field guide, a sketchbook or just the patience to sit and enjoy the sights, sounds and smells of whatever small part of the outdoors has their attention.

Trail surface conditions vary throughout the year depending on the weather, but information about trail conditions are available in regular updates from Park staff at the Visitor Centres. I've numbered the trails that are official Park trails, to correspond with Park brochures. Be sure to pick up a Park trail map before setting out. Walks without a number are not official trails but provide excellent hiking, for experienced hikers.

Trails marked with a snowflake (❄) may be suitable for skiing, depending on weather conditions and your level of expertise.

Overnight skiing in the Park requires that you register with

Official Trails in the Cape Breton

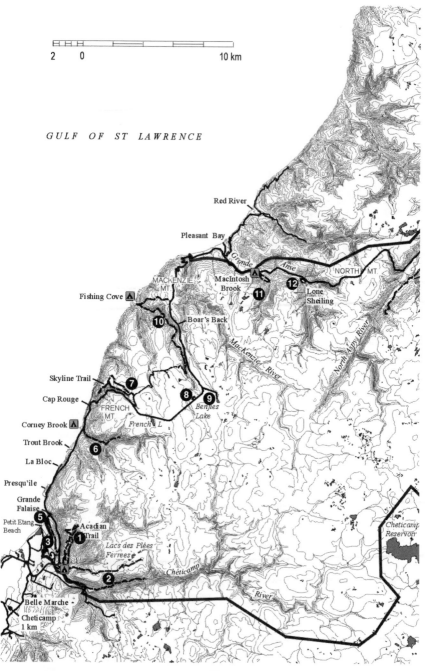

GULF OF ST LAWRENCE

Red River

Pleasant Bay

NORTH MT

MACKENZIE MT

MacIntosh Brook

Fishing Cove

Lone Sheiling

Boar's Back

MacKenzie River

North Aspy River

Skyline Trail

Cap Rouge

FRENCH MT

Benjies Lake

Corney Brook

French L.

Trout Brook

La Bloc

Presqu'ile

Grande Falaise

Petit Etang Beach

Acadian Trail

Cheticamp Reservoir

Lacs des Plées Ferrées

Chéticamp

Belle Marche
Cheticamp
1 km

River

2 0   10 km

Highlands National Park

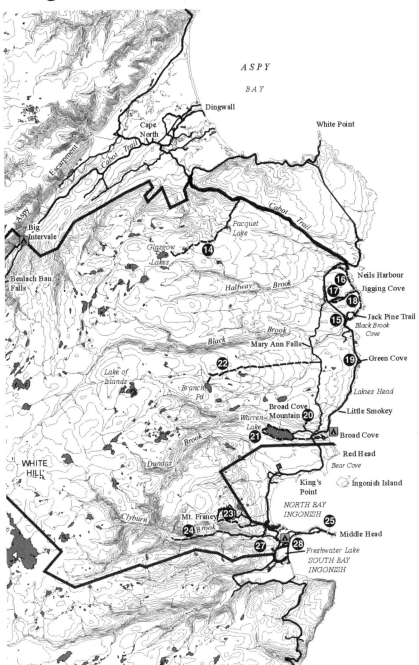

park wardens, and even for a day trip it's a good idea to let someone know where you're going. Sometimes I leave a note describing my route and time of return on my windshield or dashboard.

A word here about drinking water from the springs and small streams that are so plentiful along many of the Park's trails and throughout the backcountry. People vary in their resistance to different kinds of bugs, and for some the practice of drinking untreated water produces no ill effects. However, there is a certain risk. If you don't carry potable water, it might be worthwhile taking a water filter or tablets.

The trails are listed in clockwise order around the Park from west to east, starting at the Park entrance north of the village of Chéticamp.

Petit Étang Beach 1 km (0.6 mi) return. Level.

The gravel spit at the mouth of the Chéticamp River provides easy walking with the sea on one side, the river estuary on the other, and a sweeping view of the surrounding hills, with La Grande Falaise and the entrance to the Chéticamp River canyon visible across the estuary. The beach is suitable for swimming, and you have a choice between the ocean and the warmer, more sheltered fresh water of the lagoon. Whichever you choose, the refreshing sound and the smell of the sea will not be far away.

To get there, from the Chéticamp Visitor Centre drive south along the Cabot Trail for 2.8 km and turn right onto the paved Petit Étang Beach road. Drive 1 km and turn right onto a dirt road. Follow the dirt road for 2 km to the beach.

1. L'Acadien ❄ 8.5 km (5.1 mi) loop. A steady, moderately steep ascent for 4 km to the top of the loop (with an elevation gain of 350 m) and back down.

Spectacular views await you from the lookoffs along this trail. Hiking it counterclockwise provides the best views, and lets you do the uphill (eastern) side of the loop in relative shade. For a few kilometres the trail follows the valley of a small brook, Ruis des Habitations Neuves, up into the hills, switching back and forth across the brook on several footbridges. The ascent is fairly steep for the first kilometre or so, then it becomes more gentle. As you gain elevation the valley becomes narrower and the steep hillsides squeeze closer on either side. Near the top of the narrow valley the trail turns sharply and angles up the steep hillside, giving a grand view of the surrounding hills and tributary valleys of Chéticamp River and Robert's Brook.

Emerging upon the top of the plateau you suddenly find that the whole forest around you has changed. Down below you is the valley and the hardwood forest. But here on top you are surrounded mostly by wide open spaces. There are clumps of balsam firs and scattered birch trees, the remnants of a boreal forest that once covered most of the plateau. In the 1970s the coniferous forests of the plateau were invaded by a caterpillar known as the spruce budworm. For several consecutive years the caterpillar munched away on the new spring growth of needles on mature fir and spruce trees, finally killing the trees and wiping out its own food supply in the process.

Such catastrophic events are common in the boreal forest, and serve an important role in rejuvenating the forest. In many parts of the country, fire is instrumental in doing this job. But here on the plateau, annual precipitation is greater than any other area in the Maritimes, and in summer, low-lying clouds result in moister conditions so that the boreal forests here have been rel-

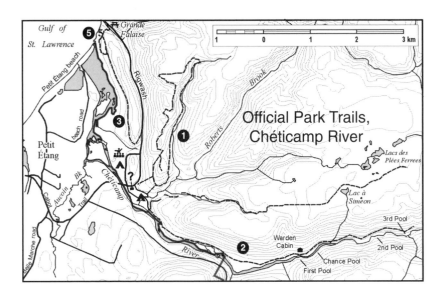

atively unaffected by fire. In its place, the ecological role of fire is fulfilled by cyclical outbreaks of insects like the spruce budworm. The insects' attacks on mature stands of balsam fir allow a variety of other plants and animals to move into the altered forest, increasing the diversity and distribution of vegetation across the landscape. In that role the spruce budworm is one of the most important animals in the Park.

Up on top of the ridge, the trail traverses a narrow portion of the plateau to a summit lookoff with a wonderful view of the coastline, hills and villages to the south, and the Gulf of St. Lawrence spread out below you to the west. From this lookoff the trail starts downhill along a broad ridge, switching back and forth from one side of the ridge to the other, giving alternate views of highlands and lowlands all the way down to the Chéticamp Visitor Centre.

About 1.5 km from the end of the trail a lookoff on the right gives you a bird's-eye view of Lac Melanie and the roadway into the Chéticamp Campground. A little further down the trail is a pit privy. The path to the left at this point goes for 300 metres to a lookoff at the top of a small knoll.

If there are clouds sitting on the summits, you won't get the dramatic views that you would otherwise, but I like to go up into these hills and walk through the fog and mist even when the visibility is not great. If the clouds happen to lift during the walk, so much the better.

The eastern side of the loop makes an exciting ski route for experienced skiers. The more exposed western side, overlooking the Gulf of St. Lawrence, has less snow cover and is rarely suitable for skiing, but if the snow is not deep it might be possible to walk it.

The trail begins a few minutes walk from the Chéticamp Visitor Centre parking lot, past the chain-link fence of the works compound, and just to the left before you come to the bridge over Robert's Brook. If you like to keep track of where you are, using a topographic map, you might notice that this trail is inaccurately placed on the map, but that shouldn't be a concern to anyone just following the trail itself.

2. **Trous de Saumons Trail (Salmon Pools Trail)** ❄ 12 km (7.2 mi) return.

Generally level except for a short (100 m), steep hill at the start and a similar small hill between Second and Third Pools.

The Chéticamp River, like most of the Park's streams, arises from the bogs, small ponds and lakes on the interior of the plateau. At first it flows in a gentle gradient, as a series of pools and riffles, not much below the elevation of the surrounding terrain. Further along it tumbles down the edges of the plateau in numerous falls and rapids, cascading through wild and beautiful gorges and deep, black pools edged with floating foam, cutting deeper and deeper into its canyon. Along the lower part of the river, the trail goes through mixed forest and beautiful, cathedral-like stands of hardwood. There's good birding along the way, too; I've counted over 25 species in a single walk. Bald eagles cruise the river, as well as great blue herons, belted kingfishers and mergansers looking for fish. I sometimes see rafts of baby mergansers motoring across the water or shooting the riffles like wind-up bathtub toys.

During the spring of 2000 some beavers built a dam on a small stream beside the Robert's Brook group campground, not far from the trailhead. By the spring of 2001 the dam had been breached and the pond largely disappeared, but you can still see the gnawed stumps and the remnants of the lodge.

A beaver dam is an extraordinary piece of construction. Made from sticks, twigs, mud, and stones, it forms a very stable structure that can withstand great water pressure. The purpose of the dam is to create a pond deep enough to not freeze to the bottom during the winter, which will provide deep-water storage for the beaver's winter food supply of sticks and twigs that he has cached down at the bottom of the pond. During the winter the beaver brings these sticks from the cache into the lodge to eat the bark. The lodge itself is made up of intertangled sticks and twigs. There are two underwater entrances, with living quarters built above the water level inside.

The beaver's lips can be closed behind the front teeth, allowing the beaver to gnaw under water without swallowing any water, and the ears and nostrils are equipped with valves that close under water. Oil glands at the base of the beaver's tail provide a waterproofing for his fur coat, and you may see them combing this oil through their fur with their clawed feet. A second set of glands, the castors, produce a scented fluid called castoreum, which is used by both sexes as a calling card on scent posts around their home territory. Castoreum holds or "fixes" the scent of any material it is mixed with. For that reason it was used as the base for perfumes.

Other places where I've seen beavers are Presqu'île Pond, Freshwater Lake and the Clyburn Brook below the Cabot Trail. Beavers are uncommon in the Park because their preferred foods such as poplar, willow and birch are not plentiful near water bodies that are suitable for beavers. This is partly because the beavers themselves have eaten most of the available food supplies, and partly because of the maturation of the forests due to the lack of recent disturbance such as cutting and fires. By the late 1800s beavers had been eradicated in Cape Breton through over-trapping. They were reintroduced to the Park in 1938 when the federal government released nine on Roper's Brook, on the eastern side of the Park.

Continuing along the dirt road through the Robert's Brook campground you come to the trailhead for the Trous de Saumons trail.

The small white building you see below you from the top of the first hill you climb houses instruments for continuously recording the water level of the river.

Along parts of the trail you can see damage to the bark of tree trunks caused from the abrasion by river ice being carried by spring floodwaters. You may see trees in other areas that have similar scars higher on the trunk but those are likely due to moose rubbing their antlers or scraping the bark off with their teeth.

When passing a certain spot on this trail I often felt a brief but sudden drop in the air temperature. It always seemed to occur at the same place, about 300 metres past where the main river first comes next to the road. I discovered that the cool, refreshing draft comes from a small cavity in the rocks of the hill-side, about 2 metres up the slope from the edge of the road. I've often found ice inside the hole in August, and to sit in front of the opening on a sweltering day is like sitting in front of an air conditioner.

The distance from the start of the trail to First Pool is 3.5 km. You will know when you're there because the pools are signed. The log cabin just beyond First Pool is a patrol cabin used by the Park Warden Service. From First Pool it's just a few minute's walk to Chance Pool, a good place to rest on the pol-ished, pot-holed rocks and watch the river run by and view the steep, rugged valley sides. From Chance to Second Pool it's 1.3 km, about a 15-minute walk. A few minutes past Chance Pool you pass on your left a long, steep scree slope of loose rock. Here one of the rare animals that the Park protects, the Gaspé shrew, hunts voraciously for bugs among the dark crannies and crevices of the jumbled rocks.

The surfaces of the river's dark pools are often laced with floating foam. The foam occurs naturally in the Park's streams, especially after heavy rains. Detergent-like compounds are re-leased in the streams by the decay of organic materials such as fallen leaves, or from organic soil material carried into the streams by surface runoff. The released compounds rise to the stream surface where they interact with the water molecules and reduce its surface tension. This allows air to mix more easily with the water. Bubbles form in turbulent rapids and waterfalls as air mixes with the interacting water and foaming agents. The light-weight bubbles congregate as foam and trace interesting swirls and patterns as they are carried along on the river's currents and eddies.

Further along, the trail passes by a small stand of hem-locks. I think if I were to rank my favourite trees, hemlock would be at the top of the list, although I'm not sure why. Perhaps I as-sociate them with scenic ravines and wild river canyons of past hikes, because that's where I find them mostly. They also tend to grow in groves, creating deep year-round shade that prevents most other plants from growing beneath them. Their uncluttered understory usually provides easy walking, even on steep inclines. There's a certain quality of light that filters through their soft branches. On hot days the spaciousness among their large trunks seems to leave room for breezes to circulate. Hemlock trees are beautiful, but the wood is of poor quality. Saw blades attempting to cut it would often break when they hit the extremely hard knots, so hemlocks in the past were saved from logging. Settlers used the tannin in hemlock bark to dye wool and preserve leather.

At Second Pool the river flows through a steep-walled, rocky gorge. If you're there during the salmon "runs" of June or July you might see one of the most thrilling sights in the Park: Atlantic salmon jumping the falls at the head of the pool.

The story of this fish is remarkable for, unlike most fish which remain in a single location for life, the Atlantic salmon is a world traveler. A salmon begins life when it hatches in the spring from one of thousands of eggs laid in the river gravel the previous autumn. Then, depending on the temperature and productivity of the river water, the young salmon spends from one to six years in the river before going to sea. Most of the salmon born in the Chéticamp and Clyburn rivers migrate after a couple of years.

Living in a sanctuary like a national park does not mean that life is easier for a little fish. The young salmon faces many challenges as it grows to adulthood, including competition for food and territory, and predation by larger fish. Birds such as herons and mergansers feed on them, as does the belted kingfisher with its bifocal vision—one phase used in the air, the other while underwater. Only one in a thousand of the little salmon make it from the river to the ocean alive.

During their stay in the river, a freshwater environment, juvenile salmon must undergo a number of physical changes to pre-adapt them for life in the salty ocean. A few behavioural changes are required, too, before they head out to broader pastures. From being territorially protective—fish with an attitude—they become more gregarious, a change that permits their migration in large schools.

At sea, salmon from both sides of the Atlantic rendezvous in the waters off southwestern Greenland, while others travel to lesser-known oceanic feeding areas. After one or more years at sea they return to the rivers where they were born. The mystery of how the salmon find their way in the ocean and eventually back to their parent river is yet to be solved. Some researchers suspect that salmon may be able to sense the gradient in electrical potential generated by the movement of an ocean current in the earth's magnetic field. Others suggest that when a salmon leaves coastal waters it comes under the influence of a rotating ocean current in which it drifts along, ultimately returning to the point at which it embarked. Like many migratory animals, they may navigate at least partly according to the positions of stars.

Many theories have also been put forward to explain how salmon are able to recognize their native streams. The most widely accepted is that they are guided by odors of the river that are imprinted on their memory during the downstream journey— odors that emanate from the plants and minerals characteristic of their home river. It is difficult to imagine how fish distributed over a vast area of open sea and moving about in it for a couple of years can converge towards the place where they first entered seawater, yet for countless generations the salmon have returned to the streams of Cape Breton Highlands National Park.

Once in the fresh water of the river, an amazing thing happens: Atlantic salmon stop feeding almost entirely until they re-enter the ocean, which may be a few weeks or as long as twelve months later. During this period the internal systems of both sexes degenerate in favor of egg or sperm production, changes that result in a loss of more than 25 percent of salmon's body weight.

Salmon spawn in late autumn. The female uses strong thrusts of her tail to dig a 10 to 30 cm deep nest in the gravel of the riverbed. Some of her eggs and the sperm of a male salmon are released into the nest, the gravel is replaced with tail thrusts and the process is repeated until all the eggs are deposited. Between 2,000 and 15,000 eggs may be laid, depending on the size of the adult salmon. The adult salmon return to the ocean feeding grounds immediately after spawning, or after overwintering in the river. Most Atlantic salmon die after spawning, but one in ten may survive their drastic loss in body weight and have enough strength to return to the sea and recuperate. Through tagging, it's been found that such vigorous individuals have returned to spawn as many as six times.

You have to wonder why a salmon would leave the rivers of Cape Breton Highlands National Park on a journey that may span more than 4,000 km of open ocean, and then return. Why not just stay in the river where you were born? The reason is that there is not enough food or space in the river to sustain so many fish. If all the salmon born in a particular river remained as adults on these nursery grounds, the resources in the river would quickly be used up. So they migrate to sea, where they can take advantage of the greater food supply to feed and grow into adults.

This raises the question of why salmon do not spend their entire lives in the sea, if feeding conditions are better there. That's because the ocean is not a good place to grow salmon eggs. Due to the low oxygen conditions in the sediments on the ocean floor, eggs buried there would not survive. Eggs laid on the bare ocean bed would have to be protected from predators or they would soon be eaten, and if the adults remained to protect the eggs, most of them would die of starvation before the eggs hatched. The aerated water and clean gravels of the Clyburn, Chéticamp and Aspy rivers provide suitable oxygen conditions and a hiding place for the eggs and larvae, and the adult fish don't have to remain in the river to guard them from predators.

Salmon need a certain depth of water below waterfalls in order to be able to jump them—about one and a half times the vertical height of the falls. In 1898 the Department of Fisheries reduced the height of the falls on Second Pool, providing access to an additional 14 km of habitat for the river's salmon. The pool below the falls here is 10 m deep—lots of runway for *Salmo sa-lar*, "the leaper."

I've never hooked a salmon. It seems to me that an animal that survives such perils during its remarkable wanderings doesn't need any more hassle from me when it comes home. Or maybe it's just that when I get on a river I want to see what's around the next bend, and I haven't got time to fish while there's new country to explore. Still, I have to admit that every time I see an angler's line go taut and hear that reel start to sing, my pulse quickens, and as I watch the leader race from one end of the pool to the other I'm always impressed at the power and speed of the silver torpedo that Izaac Walton crowned the "King of Freshwater Fish."

From Second Pool the trail gets narrower and goes on for another 300 m to where it ends at the beautifully sculpted and banded rocks beside Third Pool.

In winter the trail is used by skiers, and there is a warm-up hut with a wood stove at Second Pool.

Bicycles are permitted on this trail but cyclists should yield to hikers, especially on narrow portions of the trail, unless they volunteer to let you ride by without dismounting.

The trail begins several minutes' walk from the Chéticamp Visitor Centre parking lot. Follow the signs along the paved road past the chain-link fence outside the works compound. Cross the bridge over Robert's Brook and continue straight along the dirt road to the trailhead.

Lake Trail ❄ 11 km (6.6 mi) return. Steep ascent of 350 m for first 2.5 km through the Acadian forest. The trail becomes more or less level on top of the plateau and continues for about another 3 km through budworm-killed boreal forest before it peters out.

This used to be an official trail but it is no longer maintained. You never know what wildlife you'll see along it. The trail gets its name from a group of small lakes, Lacs des Plées Ferrées, that lie to the north of the trail. I've never been able to find out for sure what the name means. There are several meanings for the words plées and ferrées. Pascal Poirier, in his *Glossaire Acadien*, says that he has heard un plé used for un pré (a meadow), while ferrée refers to an implement such as a hoe or a spade that had a piece of iron (fer) at one end for digging. Perhaps, then, the name refers to a small piece of ground that someone had cultivated beside the brook. Another dictionary gives the following meaning for plées: "land denuded by fire; burnt." I once saw the meaning "bog" ascribed to plé and, since there are bogs adjacent to the lakes, I've wondered if the name could refer to soft, porous deposits of iron oxides known as bog iron, a poor quality ore that forms in wet areas by precipitation from iron-bearing waters and by the action of bacteria. The more I search for meanings to the words, the more possibilities I find.

There is a path to a small lake on the south side of the trail, but the group of lakes on the north side is not visible from the path. You need a map and compass to get to them.

Skiing is good after a fresh snowfall but you have to get there before the moose do, as they tend to plow ruts through the snow, and the holes made by their long legs provide an excellent means of snapping your ski poles. The trail is steep and recommended for experienced skiers only.

The trail begins several minute's walk from the Chéticamp Visitor Centre parking lot, at the same spot as the Trous de Saumons. Take the gravel road uphill to your left, just before the chain gate at the start of the Trous de Saumons.

3. **Le Chemin du Buttereau** 5 km (3 mi) return. About half a km of the trail is along a gentle to moderate incline; otherwise the trail is more or less level.

The trail leads through shady mixed woods, spruce tunnels and old fields to a fine view of the coast and lagoon at the mouth of the Chéticamp River. The trail was originally a cart track constructed in the late 1700s to link the community at Chéticamp with the remote fishing settlements of Cap Rouge. Signs along the way interpret the human history of the more than thirty Acadian families that inhabited the Cap Rouge area before the Park was established.

Before you start in along the trail, you might want to walk down the road a bit to see if there is any wildlife in Melanie Pond. I see muskrats swimming there sometimes, and black ducks tipping for food under the surface. In early June the adult ducks are followed around the pond by their brood of chicks.

This is one of those trails that seem tame enough to hikers

who are used to trekking in exotic places, but as Jerry Russel wrote, "Adventure is not in the guidebook, and beauty is not on the map." One day my wife and daughter went for a walk along this trail. My nine-year-old son had gone on ahead of them on his bicycle. When they eventually caught up to him he was lying on the ground under his bike, close to tears after being chased by a big bird. I had an idea what kind of bird might have swooped at him, and next day I took a walk along the trail. I was suddenly stopped in my tracks by a shrill scream overhead. I looked up to see the goshawk glowering at me from the top of a tall spruce tree.

I never knew a bird could look so fierce and menacing. Those weren't the cries of an anxious grouse about to pull the broken wing trick. The screams were a definite warning that I was out of bounds and I had better soon make tracks out of there, or else.

I guess I didn't move quickly enough, because as I turned to leave the hawk went past my head like a fighter jet, just brushing my hair, pulling up through an opening in the trees. It wasn't an attack, just a warning shot across the bow, but for a split second I felt something like what a rabbit must feel just before it becomes dinner. The goshawk continued flying from treetop to treetop, screaming threats. I stepped off the trail into the woods thinking, "You won't get me in here."

I figured it had a nest nearby and I started looking around to see if I could find it. Seconds later the hawk was streaking towards me, deftly side-slipping around tree trunks as it swooped on a collision course with my head. For a moment I stood in stunned amazement and waited for the bird to end its bluff and veer away. Awe changed abruptly to fear when I saw the talons swing forward, and I had just enough time to turn my head and drop to the ground as the hawk flew past and prepared for another run. I decided I could spend the rest of my life wondering exactly where the nest was and left very quickly, watching my rear all the way out.

It is customary for pairs of goshawks to return year after year to an established nest site, and this trail has had to be closed sometimes due to the aggressive defense by the birds during their nesting season.

The trailhead is at the parking lot on the Cabot Trail 1.2 km north of the Chéticamp Visitor Centre. The Chemin du Buttereau joins a loop of Le Buttereau trail (see below) by an old well. From the junction you can continue along Le Buttereau to the Cabot Trail and return to your starting point through the Rigwash Valley, making a 5.5 km loop.

This narrow valley was the site of Acadian farms until the early 1900s. Like most farms in Cape Breton at the time, they were small fishermen's farms providing for the immediate family. The old fields are growing back in now, but at the end of the 19th century a whole village existed at the mouth of the "petite source de la montagne," as Jerome Brook was called. The village was occupied in the summer by families that fished around Presqu'île and worked in a lobster cannery at Cap Rouge. The valley is supplied with numerous cold, clear springs used by the farmers to separate the cream from milk. A copper prospecting shaft from the late 1800s existed near the base of La Grande Falaise near the present highway but it was filled in after the Park was established.

The valley is sometimes frequented by bears, and from time to time you see them grazing on lush grasses and wild strawberries in the old meadows, or turning over rocks on the hillside in their search for ants and grubs. I've also seen patches of turf rolled up to expose the ground underneath, as neatly as if it had been done with a sod-cutter. Among the grasses and shrubbery of the old fields are the lavender flowers of musk mallow, a reminder of the early settlers who planted the seeds of flowers brought from the "old countries" in Europe.

Mallow, lupine and brown-eyed Susan are a few of the many flower species that made their way to the Cape Breton Highlands after being imported, accidentally or on purpose, to North America. Another example you see along the roadside, here and throughout the Park, is tansy ragwort, or stinking Willie, a noxious weed that can infest pastures and poison grazing livestock. A native of Europe and Asia, it was introduced into North

America in the 1800s. This yellow-flowered plant causes itchy eyes and runny noses among hay fever sufferers. The strikingly coloured black and orange caterpillars crawling over the foliage and flowers of the ragwort plants are the larvae of the cinnabar moth. Also native to Europe, the moth was introduced to Nova Scotia in 1961 in an effort to control ragwort. The striking moths, which fly by day, are easily recognized with their wings of dark gray and coral red.

Purple loosestrife, a pretty but aggressive alien that threatens to invade the Park's wetlands, hasn't become established in the Park yet, but it's at the doorstep. Every year, the Park's resource conservation staff monitors its advance and tries to control it with the cooperation of local communities.

The Chéticamp River once flowed through the Rigwash. During the late stages of the last glaciation a glacier in the Gulf of St. Lawrence blocked the river's present outlet and diverted its course through this valley. And as you walk along the highway you'll find evidence of a much earlier event in the Park's geological history. Along the backslopes of the ditch are dark fragments of basalt—rock from the earth's interior that belched onto the surface as molten lava. The cavities in these rocks were formed by the expansion of gases trapped in the cooling lava. Some of the cavities are filled with minerals precipitated from the volcanic gases and fluids.

5. **Le Buttereau** 1.9 km (1.2 mi) return, or 5.5 km (3.3 mi) loop. A moderate incline for the first 300 metres, otherwise the trail is more or less level.

The trail starts off uphill with a spectacular view of the face of La Grande Falaise looming through mist or towering in sunshine across the narrow valley of the Rigwash. This bold wall of rock is part of a range of hills that once lay on the other side of the Park. It was transported to its present location during a time of collision between the various geologic plates that make up Cape Breton. During the collision, some of the Bras d'Or plate was thrust far to the west of its original position on the eastern side of the highlands, and it now comprises part of an escarpment running from La Grande Falaise southward to beyond Chéticamp. This belt of rock eventually became isolated from its roots on the other side of the island by erosion of the intervening rock. You can see the escarpment from the Grande Falaise lookoff, as well as from the lookoffs further along Le Buttereau trail. Veins of gypsum and calcite near the bottom of the cliff at La Grande Falaise suggest that these minerals, buried somewhere in the highlands, may have acted as a lubricant in the relocation process.

A large cleft or "chimney" that runs up the central part of the cliff face shelters a raven's nest. You can see the nest from the trail with the help of binoculars, where the second-from-the-bottom band of black rock intersects the cleft at the top of a large patch of orange lichen. One day I watched the adult ravens ferrying food to the nestlings. What a commotion the young birds raised each time one of the adults returned. Their squawks reverberated back and forth in the cleft of the rock, which seemed to amplify the racket.

From the top of the rise the trail descends gently to a seaside bluff that provides a fine view of the lagoon of the Chéticamp River and the Gulf of St. Lawrence. Years ago the road went along the gravel spit that separates the lagoon from the ocean and there was a bridge across the mouth of the river. Remnants of the old bridge are still visible in the sand at the mouth of the river. The first bridge was built in 1880. It was demolished twice by heavy ice and reconstructed both times. The last bridge across the river here was dismantled around 1946.

The ridge on the south side of the Chéticamp River estuary, next to Petit Étang beach, is an example of a moraine—a ridge or mound of till deposited at the margins of a stagnant or retreating glacier. It can be seen from the bluff overlooking the mouth of the river.

Half a kilometre from the bluff the trail comes to a junction with the Chemin du Buttereau trail, near the old well. From here you can either turn left and make a loop back to meet the trail you walked in on, or you can turn right and continue along the Chemin du Buttereau to the Cabot Trail and return to your starting point through the Rigwash Valley, making a 5.5 km loop.

The trail passes through mixed woods and beside old fields that are the remnants of several Acadian farms that existed here before the Park was created. The farms were small and life was divided between fishing and farming. A few stone cellars can still be seen but the fields are growing back in with spruce, wild rose and spirea. Eventually the forest will reclaim them.

Bear scat and footprints are sometimes found along both of these trails, and many of the rocks beside the trail have been overturned by bears searching for ants.

Another way to return from this trail—but not an official trail—is to go down from the bluff to the beach at the mouth of the Chéticamp River and follow the rocky shore for half a kilometre back to the parking lot. It requires some scrambling over boulders, and the passage may be blocked near the halfway point by high tide or waves from onshore winds. You can check these conditions before you go by viewing the shore from the Grande Falaise lookoff just up the road.

There is an interesting assortment of rocks, both in the cliff and on the beach, some of which contain veins of white calcite and purple fluorite. The sedimentary rocks of the cliffs have been folded and faulted so much that the layers are actually over-turned, with the older layers on top and the younger ones under-neath, the reverse of the sequence in which they were deposit-ed, and in which they are normally found. Some of the rock here resembles coarse granite but it is actually a type of sandstone, called arkose, made up of fragments of eroded granite. Its quartz, feldspar and mica grains—the common minerals in gra-nite—can be easily distinguished.

Black guillemots, or sea pigeons as they are sometimes called, breed along this rocky coast. I sometimes see them flying in from the sea with small fish, which they get by diving, to the ledges on the cliff.

The trailhead parking lot is beside the Cabot Trail 3.5 km north of the Chéticamp Visitor Centre.

Presqu'île Shore

From the parking lot at Presqu'île Pond you can follow

south along the shore toward the sea stacks known as Pillar Rocks. This is a good place to relax and listen to the sounds and savour the smells of the sea or, in stormy weather, to watch the waves exploding against the rocks.

Where the barrier beach meets the cliffs are large boulders of gneiss (pronounced "nice") and coarse granite that have been dumped there to stabilize the bank below the highway. Beyond this, you walk beneath high cliffs of foliated, shiny schist. The yellowish-brown stain in the layers near the beginning of the cliffs is due to leaching of sulphur and iron. Further on the rocks contain green football-sized nodules of the mineral epidote. Near the sea stacks, the shore is accessible only at low tide, and some scrambling is required.

Beyond the stacks the shore is impassible due to the steep cliffs. The stacks are crowned by a coating of white guano deposited by cormorants that use the rocks as a roost. The plumage of these prehistoric-looking birds is not as waterproof as that of other seabirds, so they frequently must dry their feathers out in the wind. They stand here on top of the rocks with wings outspread, like laundry hung out to dry.

I've found that the waters off this beach are a good area for snorkeling. It's interesting to poke among the shoals that lie just under the surface. They form ridges and stacks where you can swim through beds of swaying kelp and see a variety of sea creatures such as anemones, stars, sea urchins, lobsters and fish.

The shore can also be followed for a short distance north from the parking lot to where coarse sandstone and conglomerate form low cliffs around a tiny cove.

In Presqu'île Pond, particularly in the larger portion on the east side of the highway, you can sometimes spot muskrats or beavers. The remains of a beaver lodge can be seen on the far shore of the pond, at the north end. Although I've seen beavers there from time to time in the last few years, there may not be enough food in the area now to keep them permanently. Otters also visit the pond occasionally. Incredibly playful and endlessly active, their silky, streamlined bodies move through the water with quicksilver speed and grace.

Presqu'île—La Bloc Shore

This shoreline offers easy walking along the sand and gravel beach beside the Cabot Trail and beside the dirt road to La Bloc. To the south, the beach curves around a small cove past a cliff with colourful, tilted layers of sandstone, and out to a rocky point that is accessible at low tide. On a calm day this point offers a wonderful place to loaf on the rocks and view the mountains rising up from the sea. Beware of patches of poison ivy between the highway and the beach. The knee-high shrub has three-part glossy green leaves. The waters around the cove and rocky point are a good place for snorkeling, and at low tide you can find barnacles, sea stars and crabs in the rock pools along the shore.

You can also find purple starfish clinging to the submerged rocks (you might have to cling to the rock as well!). The starfish looks like a rather simple animal but the animal's nervous system is elaborate. It is able to manipulate the unusual hydraulic-pressure mechanism by which it moves its many pairs of tube feet, which enables it to hold on so hard to a rock that great effort may be required to pull it off. The suction exerted by the tube feet is great enough to open the shells of clams, oysters and mussels on which it preys. However the shell doesn't have to be opened very far. An opening of only a millimetre is enough to permit a starfish to work its large stomach, turned inside out, between the two halves of the shell. In feeding, the starfish is aided by an enzyme so powerful that it can digest living tissue even after being diluted in seawater.

Starfish have the ability to re-grow an arm after they lose it. In fact, provided that there is enough left of the body region to which it is attached, a single arm may reconstitute itself into a whole new starfish.

In 1900 a lobster processing plant was built at La Bloc on the flats behind the wharf. The wharf itself was built around the same time, and originally had a T-shaped slipway on the left side for hauling boats up. This area also had a small summer village of shacks around the plant and up the hill, and remnants of the stone foundations can still be found. The lobster plant operated for about fifteen years.

People walking the dirt road have occasionally reported hearing a mysterious sound emanating from the steep, thickly-forested slopes above. It's been variously described as a repetitious knocking that comes and goes at different times during the year. Others describe it as the sound of an animal breathing heavily, or turning over rocks in the manner of a bear, and have sworn they've seen a bear there. Still others wonder if it's the ghost of some old prospector chipping away at the rocks with his hammer.

La Bloc—Cap Rouge Shore

Beyond the end of the dirt road at La Bloc, the shore is passable on foot for about a kilometre. The cliffs behind the shore here consist of tilted layers of phyllite, sandstone, shale and glacial clay. The high angle and layered structure of the rock have led to slumping of large sections of the mountainside as the sea undermines the cliffs. The instability of the slopes is evident from the beach. Higher up the slope the Cabot Trail has twice been rerouted further back when the slumping hillside threatened to carry the highway into the sea. At the end of the beach your way is blocked by a low sandstone headland, part of the old marine bench described on page 93. Here the bench is capped by a layer of beach gravel and red glacial clay. The easiest way to get to the other side of this impasse is to drive around to the Trout Brook picnic area, described below.

The structure, appearance and mineral composition of most of the rock of Cape Breton Highlands has been so affected by intense heat and pressure that it no longer resembles the original rock. The shiny, foliated rock called phyllite, exposed in these cliffs and in the roadcuts on the mountain above, was originally muddy sea-floor sediments. They hardened into shale and then were subjected to heat and pressure during the formation of the Acadian Mountains as tremendous forces of shearing, compression and folding flattened and realigned the rock's mineral grains. Heat and mineral-laden gases emanating from rising magma permeated the rock, baking it and changing its chemical structure and physical characteristics. The microfolds in these rocks are characteristic. The sheen on the rocks is caused by light reflecting off the parallel alignment of microscopic flakes of mica.

Trout Brook Shore

The shore is accessible by scrambling down the steep bank towards the brook below the picnic area. I've sometimes seen mink curiously poking their heads out from among the logs piled upon the shore at the mouth of the brook, and even run right by my feet if I didn't move around too much.

The sea stack just offshore used to form an arch, but in 1980 the roof of the arch collapsed, the victim of repeated attacks by storms and ice, a reminder that even the rocks are not entirely ageless. Ice begins to form in the Gulf of St. Lawrence in early winter, and by the end of January most of the gulf is ice covered. At its maximum, the ice pack surrounds Cape Breton Island as far as its southeast coast, and extending across the Cabot Strait to Newfoundland. Winter winds and currents in the gulf move the pack around, sometimes creating open water between the floes, sometimes forcing them together in huge pressure ridges and piling them up on shore in great jumbled rafts.

The ice becomes dotted with seals that migrate from their summer feeding grounds in the Canadian Arctic, and they can often be seen from the highway along this coast. Sometimes seals stray far from their homes on the drift ice and wander inland, for some unknown reason. One year, baby seals were found in the Chéticamp campground, and others far up the MacKenzie River. One was even spotted traveling along the highway on the plateau between French and MacKenzie Mountains. Warmer spring weather brings the disintegration of the ice and the pack begins to disperse. By late April the last of the floes, stained reddish-brown by soil blown from the potato fields of Prince Edward Island, are being carried through the Cabot Strait by the currents of the Gulf.

To the north of the brook, you can follow the shore for half a kilometre or so. It's more interesting at low tide, when a broader area of shoreline is exposed. Behind the beach are high banks of clay and glacial till where you can see the effects of the ocean's incessant gnawing at the shoreline. Here, large portions of the hillside have slumped downward from erosion by waves and ice. Further along you'll find yourself dwarfed by jagged cliffs of phyllite. The shiny, contorted rock is laced with veins of gypsum, calcite, quartz and veins of green and purple fluorite that are sometimes mistaken for amethyst.

Trout Brook picnic ground is situated on an alluvial fan, a mass of silt and till brought down the valley by glacial meltwater and spread out on the valley bottom in a characteristic fan shape.

6. **Corney Brook** ❄ 6.4 km (3.8 mi) return. Generally level with some gentle rises. It starts across the highway from the Corney Brook campground.

This Acadian forest trail goes through the shady mixed woods and groves of hardwood in the valley, and along Corney Brook to a small waterfall on one of its tributaries.

Near the beginning of the trail, on the hillside across the small gorge, there is a distinct boundary between the patch of spruce trees and the adjacent hardwoods. That part of the hillside now grown up in spruce was once a cleared field that was part of an Acadian homestead. White spruce commonly grows up in abandoned fields. It's sometimes called "cat spruce" because the pungent odour of its needles smells like cat pee.

Lucy, my wife, used to have a bad time with snakes, and for a long time they were low on her list of favourite creatures. Since then, they have moved at least up past earwigs and she has actually come to...well, not love them exactly, but admire them. "If they'd just give you some warning," she says. One summer in particular they seemed so plentiful that every time she went for a walk on a trail there would be one or more stretched across the path, ready to give her the shivers. One day as we were pushing our way through some spruce trees I even saw two garter snakes draped between the branches of a tree, strung there on the prickly needles like tinsel on a Christmas tree. They were sunning themselves just at head height, and as I went by they dropped out of the branches. At the same time I heard a shriek behind me. Lucy had encountered two more in a tree that she was brushing by. That little episode ended her hiking for the day, and pretty nearly for the rest of the summer. Later that day we were doing some rock climbing, and at one point I reached above my head to grab a ledge only to put my hand on a bunch of snakes that were using the ledge for a sun deck. I don't remember what excuse I made but, knowing that Lucy was probably not going to enjoy the thought of snakes raining down on her, even if she was wearing a helmet, we came down off the rock. We decided to go for a canoe ride. In the ocean, she insisted. But before we launched the canoe she made me do a thorough check under the thwarts and gunwales.

We've probably all heard stories of snakes, including ones about snakes that milk cows, and about the hoop snake that grabs its tail in its mouth and rolls away when danger threatens. Now that would be something to meet coming down North Mountain when you were going up on a bike! Regardless of these tales, all of the Park's snakes are harmless and non-poisonous. I've been bitten by garter snakes, the most common species, when I picked them up, but although their teeth can puncture the skin, the bite is not painful, it's like that of a kitten. They do, however, secrete a foul-smelling substance onto their captor and lash around to spread it in the hope of making a getaway when they are dropped in disgust. I must say that it works for me.

One day on the shore of Grande Anse Brook I came across a snake gliding across the rocks with a toad in its mouth. The snake was holding its head upright, and the toad, his torso buried to his armpits inside the snake, was hanging on to the snake's head with his front feet. It looked like the snake was giving the toad a ride, like one kid wheeling another along in a grocery cart. The toad didn't seem particularly concerned, or to make any effort to get out of the snake's mouth. Perhaps he didn't realize that he was groceries. Maybe he had grown up around the Buddhist Abbey at Red River and figured that it was all an illusion, just a bad dream, or maybe he had simply come to accept that he was fulfilling his role in the greater scheme of things.

Snakes become very sluggish as the temperature drops,

especially in the fall, and they're quite easy to approach. After surviving numerous encounters with snakes, Lucy is getting quite comfortable in looking at them up close, although like most of us she still gets startled when they move suddenly on a path. She has come to appreciate their variable combinations of colours, stripes and checkerboard patterns—but I have yet to see her incorporate any of the patterns into the sweaters and quilts she designs.

I see snakes most often on trails that are dry and rocky and have lots of patches of sunlight, such as L'Acadien, Corney Brook, Broad Cove Mountain and Franey trails.

Corney Brook Trail is not groomed for skiing but you can make your own track.

Corney Brook Shore

The beach below the Corney Brook campground is constantly reworked by waves driven by winds blowing across the Gulf of St. Lawrence. Storms sometimes toss up a ridge of cobblestones, blocking the mouth of Corney Brook or diverting its outflow to some new point along the beach. Heavy rains later turn the brook into a torrent that will cut through the ridge to reestablish its original course. You might come here one day and find a fairly deep swimming hole down by the bedrock that rims the south side of the brook, with the brook flowing into the ocean just beside the pool. But come back after a storm and the pool will have disappeared, and the brook will be running parallel with the beach for some distance before finding its way to the ocean under the cobblestones and gravel of the berm.

Walk along any stretch of shore in the Park and you may find the skeletons of rock crabs washed up by storms. The shells vary in size, which makes you wonder how the soft-bodied crabs manage to increase the size of their rigid armour. Before abandoning its shell, the crab grows a second, soft shell right beneath the old hard one. Then the outer shell splits and the crab backs out of the crack, taking legs, claws and even eyeballs and antennae along. Free of its old small skeleton, the crab soaks up seawater, and in a spurt of growth, increases its size by as much as

25 percent. It may eat its old shell to get calcium for the new one. The crab hides out of sight until the new skeleton hardens. Young crabs moult like this up to eight times a year, older crabs one or two times.

In the teeming world of the shore, constantly in motion, crabs are provided with means both of obtaining their food, and of avoiding becoming the food of others. Because of the possibility of being eaten or being pinned or damaged by a stone flung at them by the waves, crabs are able to sacrifice a claw so that they may survive. The claw breaks off at a predetermined point of weakness that rings each limb. From the remaining stump a new limb begins to regenerate, and with each moult and the consequent growth of a larger shell, the stump increases in size until it catches up with the corresponding one on the other side. Crabs can also regenerate new eyes and antennae.

Among the cobblestones on the shore pieces of driftwood are riddled with the tunnels of gribbles, small wood-boring crustaceans found in marine waters. They grow up to half a centimetre long. As they bore through the wood, gribbles scrape off and swallow small particles of wood and digest the fungi that live within. Because gribbles usually attack wood en masse, the wood surface quickly becomes uneven and spongy because of all the holes and cavities.

The beach is backed by glacial deposits that lie on top of a sandstone platform, which is visible at the north end of the beach. This platform, or bench, is part of an old elevated shoreline that was created over 75,000 years ago during a period of higher sea level. In periods between glaciations, sea level rose due to the water released by melting ice. During one such interval of relatively warm temperatures and high water the sea carved a new shoreline around Cape Breton Island. With the subsequent cooling of the climate and the regrowth of the ice sheets, water again became locked up in glacial ice and snow, and the sea level dropped far below the shoreline it had carved. It's estimated that the overall level of the world's oceans dropped by 55 metres. Since then, with the return to a warmer climate, worldwide sea level is again rising but the old wave-cut bench is still visible as a smooth, almost level notch that rings the island about 6 metres above current sea level. It varies in width from 1 metre to several kilometres, and in most places it's overlain by glacial till. It can be seen in various parts of the northern peninsula including Trout Brook and along the north shore of Aspy Bay. A section of the bench overlain by red glacial till is visible from the lookoffs on MacKenzie Mountain, about a kilometre north of the breakwater at the entrance to the harbour at Pleasant Bay.

7. **Skyline** ❄ 9 km (5.4 mi) return, including a 6-km loop. Generally level trail.

> Then felt I like some watcher of the skies
> When a new planet swims into his ken....
>
> John Keats

You'll have many unforgettable images to bring back with you from a walk on this trail, one of the most popular in the Park. Your hike will take you to an exposed ridge overlooking Jumping Brook ravine, with spectacular views of the surrounding coastal hills and the Gulf of St. Lawrence. Sightings of whales, moose and eagles are common from this trail, where the mountains meet the sea.

Some of the trail goes through a rather stark landscape of weathered gray snags, the remains of a boreal forest killed by spruce budworm. Once the canopy provided by the conifers was gone, the forest floor lay open to sunlight, resulting in a lush growth of shade-intolerant shrubs and deciduous trees such as raspberry, pin cherry, birch and mountain ash, just the kind of edibles on which moose thrive. With no natural predators and a flourishing food supply, moose numbers rapidly increased in the Park. An adult moose eats 15 to 25 kg (33 to 55 pounds) of grub each day, and with an estimated one to two thousand moose in the Park, their feeding has had a significant impact on the vegetation there. In the normal course of events, after a softwood forest is removed by insects, fire or disease, deciduous trees such as white birch would be expected to sprout up in the newly opened spaces taking advantage of the increased sunlight. In turn, shade-tolerant conifer seedlings will sprout under the shade provided by the deciduous trees. After 15 years or so the balsam fir trees break through the birch canopy, and in time the fir is able to crowd out all but a few birches. The remaining birches play an important role in spacing the fir trees as they continue to grow. After about 75 years the forest reverts to a climax forest of pure stands of well-spaced balsam fir.

That's the usual sequence of events. But the heavy browsing of the moose has altered this succession on wide areas of the plateau. As the moose chow down on the deciduous trees, they crop them to a more or less uniform height, creating the almost hedge-like effect that you see from the trail. It is not known for sure whether this will ultimately hasten or retard the regeneration of the conifers. And there may be another factor involved. Art Lynds is a forest ecologist with the Nova Scotia Department of Environment. He's observed that no conifer regeneration was coming up where there were pure stands of bracken fern, a pioneer species that is widespread on the plateau, and known to inhibit the growth of other species by producing a variety of chemical compounds. He notes, too, that bracken fern's vigorous roots can grow under the root systems of tree seedlings, effectively starving these seedlings of nutrients and water. Lynds wonders if these characteristics of the bracken fern could be limiting the re-establishment of balsam fir on the plateau. In any case, the moose have certainly done a number on the Park's regenerating hardwood.

Still, everything nourishes as it has been nourished, and the recycled leaves and twigs can be found in the countless pellets that cover the ground, often in such numbers that they form sort of a "fecal till."

The gravel road from the parking lot is part of an older route of the Cabot Trail. (See the section on the Old Cabot Trail near the end of this chapter.) After a kilometre a footpath to the left takes you toward the Skyline ridge. Half a kilometre along this path it divides to form a loop. I prefer to walk the loop counterclockwise. If you don't want to walk the whole trail but still want to get out to the ridge, you can eliminate about 1.5 km from the hike by taking the left branch at the split and returning by the same branch. The left branch has a smoother surface, as well. But chances are you'll miss something if you don't do the whole loop.

The Skyline Trail can be good for skiing but it tends to be windswept. Even in cloudy weather it's exciting to be up here, seemingly at the edge of space, looking down into the void. When there's lots of snow, the wind tends to build it up into snow cornices that overhang the edge of the ravine. Don't stand too close to them or you may find yourself engaged in some extreme skiing down the precipice into Jumping Brook.

8. **Bog Trail** 500 m (450 yd). Level, self-guiding boardwalk. Wheelchair accessible.

> *What would the world be, once bereft*
> *Of wet and wildness? Let them be left.*
> *O let them be left, wildness and wet;*
> *Long live the weeds and the wilderness yet.*

Gerard Manley Hopkins

One of the many interesting features of the boreal and tai-ga regions of the plateau is the occurrence of extensive areas of peat bogs. These waterlogged areas vary in size up to several square kilometres. They are fascinating places that give you a sense of spaciousness and things primeval. When the ice sheets retreated from the plateau they left behind a thin veneer of glacial till and large areas of exposed bedrock. In this kind of terrain drainage systems do not readily develop, and water tends to collect on the ground surface instead of running off. As a result, the heavy rainfall of the region is captured and reacts with the rocks, maintaining wet, acidic conditions that are condu-cive to the growth of several species of sphagnum moss. This is the beginning of a cycle, the start of an ecosystem that develops through a series of changes that merge one into the other in a process called succession.

Only a few of the cells in sphagnum leaves are used for manufacturing food; the majority of cells are for storing water. Some species of sphagnum can soak up to 40 times their dry

weight. For that reason, and because of their antiseptic properties, they were once used as hospital dressings. Rain falls upon
the bog, but instead of running away it is absorbed by the moss
and the bog swells like a huge sponge. For much of the year the
bog is saturated, so that rival plants to the sphagnum can't live
there because they can get no air. The sphagnum grows upward
and crushes its older parts down into cold, dark water, where
bacteria partially break down the dead fragments. As the organic
matter becomes compacted beneath the upward growing moss,
the substrate is turned into a nutrient-poor acid waste and the
depth of the bog becomes a pickling vat in which change almost
ceases.

The different species of sphagnum have different growth
rates and, as a result, the surface acquires an uneven topography of mounds and hollows. As the mounds build up there is a
corresponding rise in the water table. Some mounds eventually
coalesce and form ridges enclosing shallow depressions. The
compacted, impervious mounds of peat act as dams, and rain-
water forms ponds behind them. The upward growth of the
sphagnum mounds may continually elevate a bog's surface until
it is eventually above the water level of the ponds, and is no
longer influenced by seepage from them, or from the ground water beneath. Now, only rainfall supplies the sphagnum. At this
stage the surface conditions are somewhat drier and therefore
more favourable for habitation by a different group of plants such
as sedges, bulrushes and, on the driest spots, black spruce and
reindeer lichen. The sphagnum has prepared the way, so to
speak, for a succeeding group of plants that are adapted to the
drier conditions created by the sphagnum.

Within the development of the bog from one stage to another there is a repeating cycle of pond formation and filling in.
This process begins with the yellow pond lily and with algae that
grow on the bottom of the pond. Sphagnum and shrubbery begin
to grow out from around the edges, forming floating mats of vegetation that break off and sink. As this filling in continues, the
pond gets shallower, and the drowned vegetation begins to surface, eventually forming a muck that is colonized by sedges.

Further drying permits other species to live there, whose root systems continue to firm the muck. As these die off and shed their parts, litter accumulates so that a new set of conditions arise, drier conditions suitable for the immigration of yet another group of plants. This succession of plants is determined as the environment of the site is changed by each preceding group of plants—from aquatic, to muskeg, to sphagnum—and finally to the higher and drier conditions that support patches of reindeer lichen, rhodora and black spruce.

Any number of these steps can be taking place at the same time in any given bog. Trees may be encroaching at one end of a bog while elsewhere on the perimetre new bog may be formed as the shade-intolerant sphagnum invades a space where the wind has toppled a group of trees and opened the site to sunlight and flooding. Evidence of this repeating cycle of submergence and regeneration comes from the discovery of layers of buried, well preserved wood fragments, some with bark present, located in pits dug in the peat.

Sometimes the complex of mounds form a maze-like pattern among the ponds, with some of the mounds interconnecting and others forming dead-end peninsulas. As you try to wend your way across the bog you may find yourself faced with the choice of having to jump across the intervening water or muck to an adjacent mound, or retracing your steps and looking for another route. One day I was walking along the edge of a narrow pond in the centre of a large bog complex. As I squelched along through the spongy peat I suddenly sank to my thighs in a quagmire, in a spot that at first glance had appeared to be quite firm. There was a small clump of shrubbery beside the pond, barely within reach, and I was able to grab on to some branches from it that were trailing along the ground. At first the thin branches kept breaking in my hands and I wasn't getting anywhere, except deeper. I took off my pack and threw it a little distance ahead of me onto some drier hummocks of moss. As I tried to extract myself from the muck, a cow moose bolted from a patch of spruce trees a few metres ahead of me and splashed across the pond, stopping in the water on the other side to eye me suspiciously. I noticed some more movement in the clump of spruce and could make out a couple of calves standing in the thicket, whimpering and wondering what to do.

I was beginning to whimper and wonder what to do myself. I would gladly have solved their dilemma by taking a detour around them, but at that moment I was on the antlers of a dilemma of my own. I kept trying to extract myself from the ooze, feeling like an utter idiot with everyone watching me. Mama moose made a couple of calls. Whether she was beckoning to the calves or threatening me I don't know, but the youngsters must have decided that with me stuck in the muck they were pretty safe, because they soon splashed across the water after her. After watching me for a few more minutes they all took off, leaving me alone.

Obviously, I got out. After that, I watched my step and kept to firmer ground.

In spite of the blockade of food supplies imposed by the sphagnum, a few plants have found unique ways of living in the bog. They've done so by becoming carnivores. Such are the sundews which, unable to find nitrogen and rare elements among the mosses, have taken to trapping them from the air in the form of flies. Look closely at their round, red leaves and you will see they are covered with fine tentacles tipped with drops of sticky fluid. A fly that alights upon one of these leaves becomes stuck and the tentacles fold slowly about it. Days later the leaf unfolds and the skeleton of the fly lies exposed, the rest of it having been digested by enzymes secreted by the sundew.

The bogs of Cape Breton Highlands are the natural habitat of another carnivorous plant, the ingeniously designed pitcher plant. Insects are attracted by sweet nectar secretions near the mouth of the water-filled pitchers that ring the base of this odd-looking flower. The pitchers act as traps to the insects, for the mouth of each pitcher is a flap covered with hairs pointing downward into the pitcher. It's one way only, since after the insect passes through, the hairs act as spikes at its back. The only way to go now is down. The whole area becomes very slippery and footing is difficult. The insect is forced into a pool of water below. As if things aren't by this time difficult enough for the victim, the water contains a wetting agent that reduces surface tension, making it impossible for the insect to crawl upon the surface. The victim drowns, and microorganisms in the liquid disintegrate the soft matter of the insect, which is absorbed by the plant. The mound of skeletal remains found in the bottom of the pitcher is mute testimony to the trap's success.

Oddly enough, in spite of its penchant for insect meat, the pitcher plant serves as a nursery for a certain species of mosquito that lives in the pitcher for part of its life cycle. In fact, the mosquito is exclusively dependent on the pitcher plant for its reproduction: the adults fly into the pitchers where they mate and lay their eggs, and the larvae hatch and live in the broth, feeding on its suspended micro-organisms. Some larvae even overwinter in the plant, becoming frozen in the liquid. When they thaw out in the spring they transform into adults and fly away to feed and find a mate.

Another carnivorous plant found in the bogs of Cape Breton Highlands is the bladderwort. (It's beginning to sound like a bog is sort of one huge death-trap, but a plant has to do what it has to do to earn a living.) You often see the bladderwort's yellow flowers on exposed peat or in the bog ponds, but their insect-trapping mechanisms are on the stems, submerged either in the moist peat or within shallow streams or ponds. The bladderwort maintains a vacuum within the tiny bladders by pumping out water. Each bladder has a trap door, and when anything touches the trigger hairs surrounding the trap, the door snaps open, sucking in its prey. Then the trap closes. After digesting its prey the bladder resets itself by pumping out the leftover liquid.

Although these carnivorous plants are most often seen in bogs, it's not certain whether their carnivorous lifestyle has evolved in response to nutrient-poor soils or to toxic ones, for they also occur in soils that are high in poisonous elements like chromium and nickel. Both facts may be related to the plants' inefficient root systems. In bogs, where nutrients are low, efficient root uptake is not much of an asset, and in toxic soils it is a definite disadvantage. In both habitats the plants' ability to get nutrients by alternative means gives them a competitive advantage.

Standing out among the muted colours of the mosses and sedges of the bog are the showy pinks of orchids with lovely names like Arethusa, Calopogon and Rose Pogonia. Orchids are very complex plants, particularly adapted to attracting insects for pollinating purposes. Their elaborate flowers have highly specialized relationships with pollinating insects. The pollen must be correctly positioned on the insects' bodies in order for it to be transferred to another flower.

The unusual lip petal of the arethusa—also called Dragon's Mouth—serves as a platform for bumblebees that enter the flower for nectar, forcing them to pick up the orchid's waxy pollen grains as they leave. Calopogon orchids (grass pink) rely on a pigmented petal that resembles a clump of stamens and attracts insects. When an insect lands on the pigmented area the petal acts like a trigger mechanism, causing the pollen-bearing structure to swing down and daub pollen on the back of the insect. The insects then distribute the pollen grains on the next flower they visit, and pollination takes place.

Peat bogs are widespread on the plateau and form the headwaters of many of the streams that we cross in driving around the Cabot Trail. In fact it is the tannins of the bogwaters that give the streams their characteristic tea-like colour.

Keep an eye out for moose on the adjacent barrens as you walk around the Bog Trail. The boardwalk is also a good place for a moonlight stroll.

9. **Benjies Lake** ❄ 2.8 km (1.7 mi) return. The trail starts at the highway on MacKenzie Mountain.

The level trail goes through boreal forest with views of the surrounding taiga. Moose sightings are common at the lake, especially at dawn and dusk, but you might be just as likely to find one upon your return shredding a tree beside your car in the parking lot. Try stepping off the trail near its beginning and taking a short walk into the tuckamoor on your right and you'll gain new admiration for the ability of moose to move around in this kind of terrain. Since it's not a long walk to the lake, I sometimes take a flashlight so that I can linger till dusk.

The boreal forest here is dominated by balsam fir with lesser amounts of white and black spruce. The infertile, rocky soils, and the length and severity of the winters on the plateau, are factors in determining what grows here. Climatic conditions on the plateau are significantly different from the rest of Cape Breton. Lower mean temperatures contribute to a growing season that is 6 to 8 weeks shorter than in the lowlands, and in some years there may be frost every month. High rainfall on the plateau leaches minerals from the soil, and frequent low clouds reduce evaporation, which in turn prevents these minerals from being drawn back up to the surface where plants can get them. Because the fir and spruce don't have to grow a whole new set of leaves each spring, they retain a large proportion of the minerals they absorb. Their demands for nourishment are relatively low, so they are able to get by on the inferior soils of the plateau.

One of the rarest and least known migratory songbirds, Bicknell's thrush is attracting much attention from the ornithological world since its declaration as a separate species in 1995. Within Cape Breton Highlands, birders have seen or heard them along Benjies Lake, Skyline, Bog, Glasgow Lakes and Branch Pond Lookoff trails, and along parts of the Cabot Trail where there are wind-stunted forests of gnarled spruce and fir. Bicknell's thrush used to be considered a subspecies of the more widespread gray-cheeked thrush, and no one paid much attention to its taxonomic status until the 1990s, when researchers at the Canadian Museum of Nature took an interest and published their findings. The American Ornithological Union's Committee on Classification and Nomenclature examined all of the available evidence and gave Bicknell's thrush full species status with the scientific name *Catharus bicknelli.*

Bicknell's is slightly smaller than the gray-cheeked thrush and has more yellow at the base of the lower bill. A chestnut colouring on the upper tail is evident in most Bicknell's thrushes. Their songs are decidedly different, and there is no evidence of interbreeding between the two. DNA analysis indicates that the two species diverged genetically about one million years ago.

Shy and reclusive, the Bicknell's thrush is rarely seen. Its affinity for remote locations and its ghost-like appearances exasperate the most determined birders. It stays hidden amid dense thickets of tangled underbrush, seldom coming out into the open. Occasionally, the male lights on a treetop for a last call as the sun sets. A rare treat for the persistent observer is the evening flight song at dusk.

There may be as few as 2,000 breeding pairs in existence, but precise estimates are difficult because of their elusive habits. The rapid disappearance of the native forests in its winter grounds in Hispaniola and neighbouring islands, combined with the fragmentation and whittling away of its limited breeding areas, is cause for concern for the species' survival.

Where the trail makes an abrupt right turn, a former fire road continues on toward the upper reaches of the MacKenzie River. The fire road, built in the mid-1950s, went right across the Park to Mount Franey, but it hasn't been maintained for years so it has become obscure and even non-existent in places. For the intermediate skier it provides a chance to explore a little of the taiga for 4 km or so to where it starts down the steep hillside of MacKenzie River. Anyone planning to ski beyond that should have good navigation skills and be properly equipped.

10. **Fishing Cove** 15 km (9 mi) or 5.6 km (3.4 mi), depending on which of two trails you take. Both trails descend through mixed forest from 340 m to sea level at the Fishing Cove wilderness campground.

Whale watching, sunsets over the ocean, swimming, exploring the grassy hillsides and roaming the rocky headlands are some of the things that make a trip to Fishing Cove a memorable experience. You can walk down and back easily in a day, but a backcountry permit is required if you plan to spend the night at the cove.

Fishing Cove was once the site of a small community. The remnants of old foundations and cellars are testimony to the perseverance of the pioneers in this isolated glen. The first settlers were Scottish highlanders who came in the early 1800s and cleared some land around the brooks that run from back in the mountains. Ocean fishing was their main means of sustenance. Their boats were driven by sails or propelled with oars, and since no wharf would be able to stand for very long the heavy seas that sometimes pounded the cove, the boats had to be pulled up onto the shore. The settlers grew their own vegetables, raised a few cattle and sheep, ground their own grain and carded and spun their own wool. Supplies and mail were brought in by boat and packhorse in the summer, and by dog team in the winter.

Around 1897 a company from Halifax built a lobster factory and a store in the cove. It was a small operation with many of the workers coming from Chéticamp during the summer months. Lobsters were cooked in copper vats over a stone-and-brick fireplace. The firewood that was used under the stove was usually cut during the winter to be ready for spring. Each morning the fires had to be going before the boats came ashore with their lobsters. After the lobsters cooked and were allowed to cool, the tails and claws were taken off, cracked open, and the meat was extracted by picks or forks and packed in cans. The bodies were used as fertilizer in the fields. Lids were sealed onto the cans using a soldering iron to melt the lead seal. The cans were then boiled in another vat for a period of time. When the cans were removed they bulged out from the pressure inside, but they were punctured with a nail to relieve the pressure, the little holes were plugged with solder and the cans were placed back into the water to boil for another hour. At first all the steps in the processing were done by hand in this and other lobster factories around the coast, including the tedious task of picking out the meat from the little walking legs of the lobster. In later years wringers were used to extract the meat, and sealing machines were introduced.

By 1915 the descendants of the pioneer families had moved to the surrounding communities and the place was deserted except for passing fishermen who maintained fishing shanties there.

A descendant of the settlers recalls a small cemetery of

four graves marked by wooden crosses situated on the east side of the brook, but time has since hidden any evidence of them.

Two great tales of shipwreck along this coast in the 18th and 19th centuries are contained in the book *Castaway on Cape Breton*. One of them recounts the adventure of Ensign Walter Prenties who was shipwrecked in December 1780 at what is now Margaree Harbour, and with his companions made an incredible trip around the northern peninsula. The following excerpt is from Prenties' narrative:

"The place where we landed [present-day Pigeon Cove, 2 km south of Fishing Cove] was a beach about four hundred yards in length, bounded at the distance of about fifty yards from the water's edge by a precipice of at least one hundred feet in height, which enclosed it on all sides.... [The] wind came round to the north-west, and blowing very hard, the sea beat with such violence against the shore as to drive our boat twenty yards higher than she was, and to beat several holes in her bottom. Now was the time for us to feel all the miseries of our present situation; for being surrounded by precipices which prevented us from sheltering ourselves in the woods, and having so little covering, and no firing but what we collected from some pieces of timber which floated accidentally upon the shore, we could just keep ourselves from absolute freezing. The same weather continued for eight days with a prodigious fall of snow, a circumstance that added to our other inconveniences."

Samuel Burrows, in his account of another shipwreck in the winter of 1823, described how he and his companions endured cruel hardships along these precipitous coastal hills in an effort to reach civilization, "pulling ourselves up by the trees" with frozen hands and feet. Their accounts make modern mountaineering stories seem like a walk in the park.

The long trail (7.5 km) descends through mixed forest along the steep-sided valley of Fishing Cove Brook. It starts out on a section of the old Cabot Trail, which is described more fully near the end of this chapter. There are several short uphill sections on the descent and the trail is rocky and uneven in a few places. The short trail (starting 4.5 km further north on the Cabot

Trail) is considerably shorter (2.8 km) and correspondingly steeper.

Both trails descend through the Acadian-type forest characteristic of the Park's steep valley slopes. I remember a lot more mountain ash trees growing along these trails one time, but since they are a preferred food of moose in the summer, their cream-white clusters of flowers are not as common as they used to be. Black bears love their orange or scarlet berries. One September day I came across a bear that was trying to direct a berry-laden branch towards its mouth with one paw, while hanging on with its other paw to the trunk of an adjacent tree in order to keep from falling down the bank.

I sometimes make a circuit by going down the long way and coming out the short way, then following the highway back to my car (4.5 km). By coming up the short way I find that you get most of the grief over within a short time, and the walk back along the highway can be interesting. There is very little difference between the length of the long trail and the combined lengths of the short trail and the highway. If I'm lucky, a passing motorist will give me a lift. Or, if I have my bike, I leave it at one of the trailheads to ride back on. Fishing Cove itself is visible from two of the highway lookoffs on Mackenzie Mountain. Incidentally, the distant islands that you see on the horizon from various parts of French and MacKenzie Mountains are Les Îles-de-la-Madeleine, part of the province of Quebec.

I've occasionally seen lynx on both of these trails.

MacKenzie Mountain Approximately 400 m (360 yd).

Part way down the Cabot Trail on MacKenzie Mountain there are two lookoffs alongside the highway, within sight of each other, about 200 m apart, on the east side of the highway. They overlook the steep-sided valley of MacKenzie River. It's unfortunate that that there are no hiking trails here, even short ones, to take you away from the bustle and noise of the highway and the sometimes congested lookoffs, for the scenery here is awesome. Sometimes when I stop at these lookoffs I walk the short distance between them, following beside the guardrail where I can look down into the ravine. When the traffic is light I like to walk the highway all the way from the bridge at the bottom of the mountain right to the top. On the walk up, new vistas open at every switchback in the road. You get better views, of course, on the way back, and the return is easier because it's all downhill.

One day years ago I was pushing my bike up this part of the Cabot Trail, my eyes to the pavement, when I happened to look up just in time to see a car wheel come flying down the road towards me. I had barely time to push the bike to one side as I jumped the other way. The wheel whizzed by between us, caromed off the guardrail at a turn in the road, and disappeared into the woods amid the sound of crashing branches. I stood there in disbelief for a few moments waiting to see what else might be coming down the road, then picked my bike up and started walking up the hill again. When I got around the next bend, there was a long straight stretch before me, but no moving car parts in sight. A few hundred metres up the road, however, there was a pick-up truck leaning a bit to one side, and a man was walking down the hill toward me.

"Didn't happen to see a wheel in your travels?"

"Black Dunlop, wide whitewall, not much sense of direction?"

"That's her, my son."

Later that day, as I was cycling down the steep, winding curves of French Mountain, there came to mind that variation of an old hit parade tune, "You picked a fine time to leave me, loose wheel." I pulled over to a lookoff and tightened the nuts on my own wheels to make sure they weren't about to depart.

Whether you walk the road up MacKenzie Mountain or drive it, you can't help noticing something peculiar about the landscape and the vegetation of the surrounding hills. It resembles neither the boreal forest of the plateau nor the lush hardwood groves of the Grande Anse valley, only a few kilometres away. The covering of scrubby vegetation and ribs of bare rock sticking through are evidence of an event that occurred in August of 1947 when a forest fire burned most of the village of Pleasant Bay and much of the surrounding forest. It's not known for sure how it started. Some believe it was by lightning because the actual place where it began was halfway up the mountainside and virtually inaccessible. A local resident remembers seeing the smoke but not being able to do much about it. "There were no trails then, no way to get at it. They couldn't fight it. They were just praying for rain. Instead of that, it was gradually getting worse."

Families in Pleasant Bay were evacuated to Chéticamp where the Canadian Red Cross had set up kitchens and tents. A continuous watch to monitor the fire's daily progress was set up from a vantage point on MacKenzie Mountain.

The Park superintendent at the time reported that the day the fire ran through the Boar's Back, the narrow divide between MacKenzie Mountain and French Mountain: "We immediately started to get all those not fighting the fire out of Pleasant Bay. By the time the last truck had left the fire was close. Some minutes after it had left I tried to follow it to make sure it had cleared the fire front but found the MacKenzie River bridge engulfed in flames and could get no further. Fortunately the fire had not yet run up the far bank and I could see enough to be fairly sure that the truck was well in the clear."

As the fire got closer to the village men began fighting the flames with water. Fanned by a westerly gale: "The fire swept over Pleasant Bay in a matter of minutes and during that time all we could do was take shelter in the open area along the water, though some walked along the shore to the road below Jumping Brook."

Walter Moore of Red River was a fire warden at the time. He told *Cape Breton's Magazine:* "We were waiting for the fire to hit. We thought we were going to fight it. But when it hit, we couldn't do a blessed thing. You would think there were half a dozen trains coming through. We had to make for the shore. Only way you could get your breath was right down at the ocean. I saw all kinds of animals on the beach—rabbits, a partridge with all the feathers burned off him—it was just wicked."

Houses exploded and roofs caved in as the fire spread.

The same gales that whipped the flames created heavy seas along the coast, and fishing boats that dared approach through the waves were met by burning driftwood along the beach.

After the fire swept Pleasant Bay it was even more spread out and unmanageable than before. Willard Hinkley of Pleasant Bay remembers, "We were there eleven days fighting it. You'd think it was under control, and the first thing you'd know, bang-o, away it would go again. Some nights you'd be up all night."

"Another day," he recalls, "a strip came through—a strip two or three hundred feet wide from the burnt part down—and the rabbits and the deer were just running ahead of that. You could see those rabbits going, boy, just sizzling."

In total the fire destroyed 10 houses, 18 barns, a school, a church, a store and about 17 square kilometres of forest. Most of the MacKenzie ravine was burned to bare granite slabs and ridges on both sides from the coast to about 5 kilometres inland.

The fire burned for two weeks and it was only with the help of heavy rains that it was eventually brought under control. Today the sparsity of the forest cover still leaves large parts of the bedrock visible.

11. **MacIntosh Brook** 1.6 km (1 mi) level loop with a 250 m side trail to a waterfall.

There are times when driving through the Grande Anse valley that the textures and colours of the forest make you want to stop your car and soak in the magic—it's just that unreal. In spring the buds and catkins create an intricate tapestry of delicate pastel tones superimposed upon the white and gray boles of the trees. The scene is equally stunning in mid-October when the explosion of fall colours reaches its peak.

The short trail beside MacIntosh Brook takes you on a peaceful walk along a snug valley to a small waterfall. The foundations along the trail are those of a sawmill that was built by a Scottish settler around 1890, and operated until 1916. To provide water power to the mill, a log dam was built upstream, and from it the water of the brook was run down a long wooden chute to operate a 3-metre-high water wheel. The water poured into large wooden buckets fastened to the wheel which, through a system of cogs, turned a circular saw. Other foundations nearby supported a house and a barn.

One day, in the brook just below the falls, I discovered a tiny water wheel that someone had made and placed there. It had been carefully put together from pieces of sticks and other debris from the forest floor and put in a quiet part of the stream, where it was held in place by a few stones. How long it turned in the gentle current, I don't know, but I hope a lot of other people got to see it before it got carried away in the next rain.

The forces of gravity have greatly influenced the forest composition here and in other valleys throughout the Park. Slow, down-slope creep of soil and rubble from the steep valley sides results in the distribution of organic deposits and materials suitable for the development of rich soil at the lower slopes and valley bottoms. Underneath the forest, the bottom of the valley is filled with glacial deposits of boulders and gravel. These have been planed into step-like terraces at different levels along the valley sides as the stream changed its course from time to time. The terraces and the little ravines that cut through them create an interesting backdrop along the walk.

If dusk finds me in this area I often hear the call of the barred owl resonating throughout the valley. Its call is distinctive: *Hoo, hoo, hoo-hoo; hoo, hoo, hoo-hooaw*—commonly translated as *Who cooks for you, who cooks for you-all?* The *hoo-aw* has a gargling sound, as if the owl needs to clear his throat. I have also heard them make some very un-owl-like sounds, including a raspy *Tseeeeet.*

I sometimes make excursions in the Park after dark, on foot and by bicycle, using a headlamp to light the way, and I'm always amazed at the number of animals that are about at night. Jumping mice, shrews, frogs, toads, owls, insects, the occasional flying squirrel and unidentified pairs of eyes show up in the headlight beam.

Moths are often attracted to the light, and I suppose the middle of your forehead may not be an ideal place to mount a lamp when you're cycling. The beam just seems to funnel them right toward your face. Bats, too, flutter in the darkness, pursuing insects, and their erratic flight frequently takes them inside the headlamp's cone of light. Although the bats come perilously close to my head and seem to be flying out of control, they always manage to dodge at the last split second and I have never collided with one.

The little brown bat is a summer visitor to the Park and I often see one or more of them at night around the lamp post near the campground entrance, where the light creates a sort of bat Burger King by attracting moths and other insects. You can watch a little drama between predator and prey there as the bats scoop the bugs out of the air with their tail membranes. If you are alert enough you might also see some moths turn abruptly even before a bat comes into view, as if they can hear the bats coming. Some moths can, in fact, detect the pulses of sound produced by the bat with a pair of specialized sound receptors, one on each side of their body.

The bat emits high-pitched squeaks, too high for humans to hear, but still quite intense, and the echoes that the bat hears as these sounds are reflected allows the bat to avoid obstacles and determine the location of its prey. With its "ears" a moth can tell from the loudness of the sound whether a bat is coming toward it, and from the direction of the sound it can tell whether the bat is above, below or off to the side.

The bat can only detect moths within range of about 3 metres, so, given enough warning, the moth can make itself difficult to capture. If the moth detects bat sound to one side or the other, its nervous system is stimulated to cause the wing muscles on that side to beat harder, steering the moth away from the bat. Once the moth's ears are being equally stimulated the moth will be oriented away from the bat, exposing less wing surface and echo-reflecting area than if it were flying at right angles to the bat. Chances are that the moth will remain undetected if it can stay out of range for a few seconds and hope that some other morsel will attract the bat's attention.

If a bat detects a moth within its 3-metre detection range, it is futile for the moth to try to outrace the bat. In this situation the intensity of the sound from the bat elicits a different response. The moth's brain is programmed to shut down its steering control system so that its wings beat out of synchrony or not at all, and the moth reverts to wild loops and dives that make it difficult for the bat to intercept it. In this mode the moth does not know where it is going, but neither does the pursuing bat! A moth that successfully power dives to a bush or grassy spot is safe from further attack because the echoes coming from the leaves or grass at the crash landing site mask those from the moth itself.

12. **Lone Shieling** Grande Anse valley at the foot of North Mountain. 1 km (0.6 mi) level self-guiding trail through an old-growth hardwood forest, with a replica of a Scottish crofter's hut.

Today I have grown taller from walking with the trees.

Karl Baker

This is a lovely, quiet place of murmuring brooks and shady trees, a place to really slow your pace and drink in the tranquillity. One of the most important and outstanding features of the Grande Anse valley is its old-growth hardwood forest. Have you ever looked into one of those stereoscopic "Viewmasters" and felt you could walk into the three-dimensional images that it creates? That's the impression I get entering these woods. This is one of the finest undisturbed stands remaining in the Maritime Provinces and has been recommended as an ecological reserve by the International Biological Program. Here, and in other undisturbed parts of the valley, you can see how a forest will grow if left to its own devices. Many of the magnificent sugar maples were seedlings in the 1600s.

The rustic stone hut at the site is a tribute to the Scottish crofting life of many Cape Breton pioneers before they emigrated from Scotland. A croft was a small allotment of land that was worked by a peasant tenant. The name shieling refers both to the summer pasture in the hills where the crofters took their animals to graze, and to the huts they built there out of stone and turf. Originally the crofting lands of the Highlands and Islands of

Scotland were owned communally, with subsistence farming carried out on a cooperative basis. After the mid-1700s the lands fell into the hands of an aristocracy who found that they could derive a greater profit by clearing the land of people and raising sheep, and by converting it into hunting estates. The new landlords squeezed the crofters off the land with exorbitant rents and by forced evictions during the infamous Highland Clearances. It was some of these exiles who first settled in the Grande Anse valley in the early 1800s. A descendant of the pioneers, Donald MacIntosh, a native of Pleasant Bay, bequeathed the land about this site to the government as the nucleus for a national park, with the wish that a shieling should be constructed on it as a memorial to the settlers and to Old Scotland. The hut was erected in 1942. The inscription on the nearby cairn reflects the Highlanders' longing for their homeland:

> From the lone shieling of the misty Island
> Mountains divide us, and the waste of seas—
> Yet still the blood is strong, the heart is Highland
> And we in dreams behold the Hebrides.
>
> The Canadian Boat Song, anonymous

If I hadn't been looking right at the ground I probably wouldn't have seen it—a little hairy pinball about the size of a grape. I say pinball because of the way it changed direction so abruptly without changing its pace, darting frenetically here and there, in and out of crevices, over and under sticks and stones, and because it seemed to propel itself along without any obvious means of locomotion—like one of those wind-up toys you might find in a novelty shop. But from the pointy proboscis that stuck out of its front end, and the zipper-like track it left across patches of snow—a track about as wide as a human thumb—I knew it was a masked shrew.

Shrews are the smallest mammals of Cape Breton Highlands National Park. The rare pygmy shrew, the smallest mammal in North America, and one of five species found in the Park, weighs in at only about 3 grams. A penny is heavier. That claim to fame creates a problem for these little creatures, because the smaller the animal is, the greater is its body surface compared to the size of its heat engine. Such a combination requires a high metabolism, and three times its body weight in grub, in order to maintain its body temperature. The masked shrew's heartbeat is over 800 beats a minute, considerably faster than that of a hummingbird. They spend their whole lives in a frenzied search for food, moving so fast and burning up energy so quickly that without food they would die in a day. When food is temporarily scarce they'll even absorb part of their brain and skeleton. At such a pace the miniature dynamos burn out after about 18 months.

Cape Breton Highlands protects what is perhaps the least known of all Canadian mammals, the Gaspé shrew. It is the only shrew whose distribution lies entirely within Canada, and the total area of its distribution is among the smallest of any North American shrew species. It is known in only three areas in the world: the mountains of the Gaspé Peninsula, a mountainous region of northern New Brunswick, and the highlands of Cape Breton Island. Researchers in the Park have found them in the Chéticamp River valley, here in the Grande Anse valley and on South Mountain.

Most of these separate populations appear to be restricted to limited areas of mature forest on scree slopes. The flattened skull and long snout allows the shrew to get at food like insects and spiders in the narrow crevices of the rocks where larger shrews cannot get. The long tail serves as a balancing aid in climbing about its rocky habitat, and its small slender body is well adapted to hunting deep within the smaller cracks and fissures of their subterranean environment.

Climatic change in prehistoric times may have reduced the range of the Gaspé shrew to the present distribution of isolated populations. Because its range may be shrinking, it is increasingly important to protect known populations from disturbance, as it is possible that they could be wiped out by severe disturbances such as fire or clearcutting. Although there is not much awareness of its existence or status, the Gaspé shrew may be the most significant mammal found in the Park.

Aspy ❄ 10 km (6 mi) return. Old fire access road through hardwoods and mixed woods.

Before the Park was established in 1936, much of its Acadian forest was disturbed by farming, fire or logging, and is no longer the "forest primeval" of the 17th century. These disturbed areas are now in varying stages of regeneration and, protected here in the Park, they will some day regain their former splendour. Some of the old-growth forest still exists in parts of the Aspy valley.

The dirt road to Beulach Ban Falls was once bordered by farms, and remnants of the old fields can still be found. Pure stands of white spruce occupy land that was once cleared on both sides of the road. Beyond the end of the road at Beulach Ban Brook, signs of human habitation become less evident. The trail beyond the brook is no longer maintained, and to get to it you have to scramble down the stream bank and up the other side. The shady trail follows the valley in a gentle gradient for approximately 3 km, then ascends more steeply up the valley side where it ends before reaching the top of the mountain. The first four kilometres or so go through spacious stands of mature hardwoods. Large yellow birch trees are common here, along with maple and beech. The lustrous, smooth, yellowish-bronze bark on the limbs and young trunks of the yellow birch gives the tree its name. Scratch and sniff the bark of its twigs and you get a pleasant wintergreen aroma.

As you ascend the steeper part of the trail the hardwoods give way to mixed woods, and rounding a bend you suddenly find yourself in an area of stunted firs with a fine view of the valley and the long, straight escarpment of the Aspy fault running as far as you can see in either direction.

The trailhead is at the end of the Beulach Ban Falls road, which turns off the Cabot Trail at Big Intervale warden station. A short side trail from the parking lot takes you to the falls. The Gaelic word beulach refers to a gap or gorge of a mountain; ban is Gaelic for white. The falls were no doubt named by the early Highlanders—the Campbells, MacGregors and Urquharts—who settled along this road. The name seems a misnomer in dry weather when only a small flow of water comes through the gap, but after periods of rain the falls become a white cascade, visible from the lookoffs on North Mountain across the valley. Next to the parking lot for the falls there was once a water-powered saw-mill shared by all the settlers of that part of the valley.

In winter the road is not passable by vehicle but is used by skiers in conjunction with the Aspy trail.

The Aspy trail and the nearby Big Intervale campground are good places to listen for owls towards dusk. The barred owl is the most common but you may hear the great horned owl as well. Both owls will answer to a human's hoots, especially in the spring. They are most active at night, preferring to remain out of sight in a tree during the daytime. If an owl happens to be discov-ered in its perch by crows, the crows will harass the owl. I saw this happen one day near the Big Intervale campground. Upon discovering an owl a couple of crows set up such a commotion that all their friends and relatives for miles around seemed to have congregated for the mobbing. They kept diving repeatedly at the owl and screaming bloody murder until it left. But even as it tried to fly away, the harassment and bombardment of insults continued, forcing the owl to take to land again. Every so often the owl would brave its tormentors to make another dash along the mountainside before taking refuge in the trees. Even after more than half a kilometre of this I could still hear the din.

14. **Glasgow Lakes** ❄ 9.5 km (5.7 mi) return; 200 m eleva-tion gain.

The trail ascends through mixed woods, fire barrens, scrub boreal forest and taiga, providing broad views of the surrounding hills, valleys and plateau. In autumn these heath barrens are a stunning exhibition of colours: the blazing crimson of blueberry bushes, the feathery yellow needles of tamaracks, the golden-brown of sedges, the deep green of the firs, and the ponds re-flecting the intense blue of a crisp autumn sky. The effect is glori-ous when the heath plants are back-lighted in a late-afternoon or evening sun. Nature just never seems to err in coordinating her colour schemes. Away to the north, the long range of the Aspy escarpment provides a purple backdrop. St. Paul's Island, known as the Graveyard of the Gulf because of its many shipwrecks, is visible on clear days beyond Cape St. Lawrence. Some believe that it was along those coastal hills that John Cabot made his first landfall, over 500 years ago.

The rocky knoll at the end of the trail is a good place to sit and drink in the scenery. One afternoon as I was making my way up the last few steps of the path toward the top of the knoll I was suddenly confronted by a number of large duck-like heads moving about on long stalks, just behind an outcrop at the crest of the hill. It was a startling sight, but after a few more steps I realized that the heads were attached to a flock of Canada geese who were just as alarmed as I was. After waddling around in confusion for a bit in the hollow amongst the rocks, they took flight and headed off for a distant pond.

Another day I was here I had the pleasure of the company of ravens. There was a stiff breeze blowing, and as I walked around the hilltop the ravens yawed, soared, stalled, tumbled and chased after each other in the wind. Every once in a while I heard a swoosh of wings just behind my head as one swooped toward me from behind and pulled up and away at the last second. You can't tell me that they weren't enjoying themselves. Scientists say that ravens are among the smartest birds in the world. They are very social, and produce a greater variety of recognizable sounds than any other animal except humans, including the familiar wooden croak and the impressions of other birds. Birder Frank Robertson of New Waterford described its uncanny watercall: "I do not know if there is such a thing as a wooden temple-bell but for me this describes the beautifully haunting call I hear coming from a soaring raven."

The raven's vocabulary also contains sounds that mean "Soup's on!" to other ravens, for whenever one bird finds a food source (namely, anything edible) he will signal loudly to spread the word to other ravens in the vicinity. Now, you'd think that, for all their intelligence, if a raven found a delectable carcass, he would just shut up about it and eat. However, there is something to be said for sharing the wealth. Alone, a raven engrossed in a meal could be taken unawares by a predator, but in a group, the companions will take turns to stand by and watch for intruders while the others eat. Thus, the whole group benefits, including the individual who issues the invitations. Now, I'm not suggesting that ravens actually think this through whenever they are about to dine, but I think there's a lesson here.

Spruce grouse, or spruce partridge as they're sometimes called, like this boreal landscape, too, with its mix of coniferous forests and open barrens. They stay up here year round instead of migrating. In summer the grouse stays on the forest's mossy ground, eating snowberries, fern tips, and the occasional spider. In winter they stay up in the trees, where they fuel their body through the brutal weather by feeding on conifer needles. On winter nights they roost either on the snow beneath spreading spruce boughs, or plummet headlong into a "snow roost" to take advantage of the insulation provided by the snow. When flushed, the grouse will often flutter into a nearby spruce tree and sit motionless, depending only on its coloration for protection. It will often let you get quite close before flying off, a behaviour that allowed hunters to walk up to it and bag it with a stick. "The only duck I ever shot was a partridge, and I killed he with a stick," an old Newfoundlander said to me once. Spruce grouse are now protected in Nova Scotia.

In winter the trail and the road to Paquette Lake provide ungroomed access to the interior of the Park. Beyond Paquette Lake the trail is quite exposed, and skiing conditions can be difficult. Drifting snow on the barrens can often make the trail easy to lose. The trail is recommended for intermediate to experienced skiers with appropriate skills and equipment.

To get to the trailhead travel 4 km south past the intersection of the Cabot Trail with the South Harbour road, then take the dirt road on the right for 1.8 km. If you're traveling in the opposite direction, go north past the turnoff to Neil's Harbour for 9 km and take the dirt road on the left for 1.8 km.

15. **Jack Pine** 2 km (1.2 mi) loop. Some short steep sections with steps. Otherwise, gentle to moderate inclines.

Although this is only a short trail, it's one of my favourites. It winds to the sea through stands of spruce, fir and jack pine, across broad exposures of glacier-scoured bedrock, and emerges on coastal headlands to the cry of gulls, that wonderful smell of crowberry and the salt tang of the sea.

Jack pines grow in areas of dry, rocky ground on the eastern slopes of the Park that were once swept by forest fires. In fact, this species is largely dependent on fire for regeneration. The seed cones may remain dormant on the tree for more than 25 years, until the heat of such fires causes the seeds' release and generation, resulting in an even-aged stand.

The trail begins at the parking lot adjacent to the Black Brook day use area.

16. **Coastal** 11 km (6.6 mi) return (9 km loop if you return via the highway). You can modify the route by using the Jigging Cove Brook Trail (see below). The trail is more or less level but it goes up and down in a few places to get around cliffs and over small headlands.

The trail winds along the coast beside windswept spruce, across cobblestone berms and rocky headlands, where the fragrances of bayberry and crowberry mingle with those of seaweed and wild rose. It's almost intoxicating. On some days you can savour the smell of low tide as you explore vividly coloured tide pools spread like miniature gardens on the rocky ledges, while offshore the gentle surface waters sparkle in the sun. On other days the very foundations tremble beneath your feet as storm-driven surf pounds against a granite buttress, flinging its spray against the sun or rebounding out to meet the incoming waves, trailing a wake of translucent green inlaid with a filigree of white foam.

Instead of following the footpath, I sometimes prefer to scramble along the ledges and among the boulders near the water's edge. The rock is interesting along here—a foliated metamorphic rock called gneiss. It is exposed all along the coast from Neil's Harbour to Green Cove, and in the roadcuts along the Cabot Trail. Gneiss is the banded rock that shows layers of granular minerals such as quartz and feldspar alternating with darker layers of platy minerals such as mica and hornblende. Much of the gneiss has been intruded by granite magma. Some parts of it have drifted off and become engulfed and partly digested by the molten granite. Other parts have been injected with criss-crossing veins and sheets of molten granite to form a composite rock with a composition somewhere between the original gneiss and the granite.

There are two trailheads. One is across from the parking lot at Halfway Brook and the other is at a parking lot adjacent to the Black Brook day use area.

The Halfway Brook parking lot is near the former site of the halfway house that was operated by the provincial government as a refuge for travelers along the road from Ingonish to Cape North. If you follow the dirt road from the parking lot into the woods for about 150 metres and turn right onto another path, you will be on the remains of that old road. The halfway house operated until 1912, after which it was torn down and the materials used by a local resident to build a barn in Neil's Harbour, where it is still standing today.

The old road that continued to Cape North fell into disuse after a fire swept through the area in 1921. The fire was started by prospectors several kilometres back in the hills where they were analyzing mica deposits for possible commercial production. The thin transparent sheets of mica, known as isenglass, were used as fireproof windows in coal stoves. A cart track had been built to bring the mineral to Neil's Harbour where it was shipped to North Sydney. The prospectors had been blasting test holes. A campfire, allegedly set to keep away mosquitoes, spread after the prospectors left and burned for a week, threatening the communities of White Point and Neil's Harbour. In Neil's Harbour two sawmills and three homes burned to the ground. The fire eventually extinguished itself when the wind changed direction.

17. **Jigging Cove Lake** 2.2 km (1.3 mi) loop around a small lake. Mostly level except for a short hill of 50 m length.

Autumn is my favourite time of year to walk this trail. On a sunny day the contrast in colours between the dark green spruce, the scarlet red maples and the brilliant blue of the lake provide good opportunities for fall photography.

18. Jigging Cove Brook 7 km (4.2 mi) loop.

This route takes you partly along the Coastal Trail (16) and the Jigging Cove Lake Trail (17). A 1.2 km path (moderately sloping and a little rocky) connects the two trails, providing a loop that includes the highway between trailheads. You can start at either trailhead.

19. Green Cove 200 m (180 yd) return.

This short trail leads across a bare granite headland jutting into the sea. It's a good place to bask on the rocks and listen to the call of the seabirds and "the good, strong sea, the salt, bitter sea that could whisper to you and roar at you and knock your breath out of you." Green Cove was once the site of a small fishing hamlet. As the population of northern Cape Breton grew in the 19th century, fishing became the mainstay along the coast, and in order to be close to the fishing grounds, fishing stations and shanties were established on remote parts of the coast such as Green Cove. Some fishermen would stay in the shanties, returning home only on Sundays, while others made more permanent dwellings in some of the tiny coves. Green Cove was occupied on a seasonal basis from around 1880 to the Second World War. Families from Neil's Harbour and Ingonish would move here in the spring and early summer and remain until fall. Some families may have stayed here year round, for at one time the cove had its own school and post office. With the advent of the gasoline engine fishermen no longer had to row to get to the fishing grounds and, like most of these isolated hamlets, Green Cove was abandoned as the fishermen moved closer to their villages.

Black Brook—Little Smokey Shore

The shore to the north and south of Green Cove is a combination of cobblestone beaches, exposed bedrock and cliffs, and is accessible from the highway in several places. You can dance your way from boulder to boulder between Green Cove and Black Brook or Lakie's Head and, if you're a little more athletic and like the feel of solid rock underfoot, there's good scrambling from Lakie's Head to Little Smokey. Lakie's Head is misnamed on current maps. In the days when Green Cove was an active fishing community, a trail led from Green Cove to this point of land which was known as Ladies' Head. Apparently it was a popular courting place for the young people of Green Cove, where they went to "watch the submarine races," so to speak. Hence the name.

20. **Broad Cove Mountain** 2.4 km (1.4 mi) return. Short but steep or, if you wish to look at it another way, steep but short.

The trail switchbacks up the mountainside through mixed woods to a panoramic view of hills, sea and sky. Below you are spread Warren Lake, Broad Cove campground, and the long, sandy crescent of the North Bay beach. Bald eagles can often be seen here soaring on updrafts rising from the valley. Across the waters of the bay lies Middle Head, and in the distance the distinctive promontory of Cape Smokey merges with ranges of forest-clad hills to the west.

To your right the steep-sided valley of Dundas Brook emerges from somewhere back in the highlands. The hills themselves remind me of ones you might see in a diorama or in model railroad displays, with a fleece-like carpet draped over them. On sunny days the shadows of clouds creep over their textured surface, wrapping themselves around the folds, racing down the contours of the hills and gliding up to their crests again. At your feet, between outcrops of granite bedrock, are patches of sheep laurel and of reindeer lichen. Around the lookoff spruce, fir and wind-blown pines pierce the backdrop of sea and sky. To your left, beyond the horizon, lies the coast of France.

You can sometimes see the Newfoundland ferry making its daily voyage across the Cabot Strait.

To get to the trail, drive along the Warren Lake road for 500 metres. The trail starts on your right, by the sign.

21. **Warren Lake** ❄ 5 km (3 mi) loop around Warren Lake.

This level trail goes through mixed woods with views of the lake all along the way. The 40-metre-deep lake, the largest in the Park, was formed thousands of years ago when glacial deposits dammed the valley. The sandy deposits now form an excellent beach near the picnic area beside the trailhead.

Loons are commonly heard on Warren Lake, and if you see any the Park Warden Service would be happy to hear from you. You should note the time, how many you saw and what they were doing (feeding, swimming, preening, or calling). Their ages can be roughly determined by their appearance: downy young are less than one third the adult length, covered in dark gray or black down, and they may be riding on their parent's back. Larger young have a lighter, more mottled plumage of down or feathers, and will not be on their parent's back.

It's interesting to note that in 1959 Warren Lake was poisoned by limnologists to eliminate eels and perch and to prepare the lake for stocking by the "more desirable" species of speckled and rainbow trout. The following winter 10,000 speckled trout from the fish hatchery in Margaree were released through holes sawn in the ice. In 1961, 48,000 rainbow trout, raised in the Margaree hatchery from eggs shipped from Washington state, were added to the lake.

Two other water bodies in the Park, Freshwater Lake and Presqu'île Pond, were similarly stocked with this exotic species.

Today, with the emphasis Parks Canada places on maintaining ecological integrity, fish stocking no longer takes place except where necessary to restore native species that have been adversely affected by changes to their habitat by humans. This reflects a broader policy of minimal interference to natural processes, with manipulation of these processes being permitted only where they have been altered by humans, and the manipulation is required to restore the natural balance.

Even where native plant and animal species are reintroduced to a national park, it can only take place after scientific research has shown that there won't be any adverse effects on the Park or on neighbouring lands.

The 1.5 km road is not plowed in winter, but it is groomed for cross-country skiing.

To get to the trail, take the dirt road from the Cabot Trail 400 m north of the Broad Cove campground. You can also walk to it via a 1.3-km path beginning across the road from the entrance to the Broad Cove Campground.

Mary Ann Falls ❄

Short trails on both sides of Mary Ann Brook lead to observation points overlooking the falls and the gorge below. The pools at the falls are a good place to take a plunge on a hot day. I've been at the falls after periods of prolonged heavy rain when they become a raging cataract, and the pool at the bottom is covered by a layer of white froth a metre deep—an interaction of organic compounds with the water, as described on page 75.

To get there turn onto the Warren Lake road 400 m north of Broad Cove campground, and take the first dirt road to your right. The gravel road takes you to the falls after 6 km. This road was once part of the old Cabot Trail between North Ingonish and Neil's Harbour. During the late 1940s and early 1950s it was relocated and rebuilt along the present more scenic route along the coast. For a description of the old road beyond the falls see the notes on the Old Cabot Trail, at the end of this section on hiking trails.

22. **Branch Pond Lookoff** ❄ 8 km (4.8 mi) return to Branch Pond lookoff. This former fire road, built in 1952, extends beyond the lookoff but is not maintained. Gradual ascent of 300 m over the first 6 km, followed by minor dips and rises. Mountain bikes are permitted. The trail is often wet in places, especially in late spring.

The first 3 km of the trail starts out through a scrub boreal forest. At first it doesn't provide much of a view, but as you gain elevation and the forest gives way, the scenery begins to unfold and becomes more interesting. At the higher elevations, and the further inland you go, you find yourself in areas of the central plateau that are devoid of forest, with broad stretches of taiga—a transition area between boreal and tundra landscapes—extending across the rolling terrain. Here are rocky knolls, small lakes and ponds, muskeg and broad areas of heath "barrens" in which reindeer lichen, sheep laurel, rhodora, tundra birch and several species of arctic-alpine plants grow.

The low vegetation in these open spaces provides sweeping views across the slopes of the plateau. The failure of forests to develop in these barrens is largely due to poor soil conditions and to the combined influence of snow and wind during the winter months. Heavy winds prevail across the taiga, especially in winter, when it blows the snow from the more exposed sites and piles it up in the sheltered places. Exposed hill crests may be swept entirely bare, while in some of the ravines great drifts fifteen metres in depth may accumulate. I've seen snow in some of these ravines on the first of August in some years.

In exposed situations any tree branches which project above the surface of the snow are liable to be killed by excessive drying or through the blasting action of the wind-driven snow. The severity of the weather results in an aborted attempt at forest development, rather than true forest. There may also be another factor involved in the formation of these scrub barrens. It's been found that many of them are underlain by an impervious layer of soil that is not really conducive to forest growth. The compacted soil may have been formed under the weight of former glacial ice.

Three species of trees predominate in this scrub forest: balsam fir, black spruce and tamarack, and they each have found ways of surviving the elements.

Balsam fir stubbornly persists in sending up a new leader or growing tip every time a leader is killed, continuing the upward growth of the trunk, while its side branches tend to spread out laterally, low to the ground. More than twenty dead leaders have been counted on a single tree. Trees with trunks up to 40 cm thick may be less than two metres tall, and often the total height of the tree may be not much greater than that of its stubby trunk. Some such trees are over 200 years old. You can see trees here and there rising a couple of metres above the general level of the surrounding vegetation that have had all their foliage blasted away except for a small crown at the very tip.

The black spruce behaves differently. Upon the death of its primary leader, nearly all the side branches develop new leaders, giving the spruce a bushier, more prostrate appearance than the fir, and a tree devoid of a distinct trunk. (To tell the difference between fir and spruce: on fir trees the needles are flat and stalkless, arranged more or less on opposite sides of the twigs. The cones are upright. Spruce needles are four-cornered and spirally mounted on tiny pegs. Their cones hang down.)

The tamarack seems to be better able to stand the rigorous winter climate. Although it becomes gnarled and scraggy, it is seldom killed back to any extent. The tamarack is notoriously intolerant of shade, and in most places it gets crowded out in competition with more shade-tolerant species. It's only in open places like swamps and these barrens that this stalwart tree carries on. Although the tamarack is a conifer like spruce and fir, it is not an "evergreen"; it sheds its feathery needles each fall in a showy burst of yellow.

Many parts of the taiga are covered in low, dense, impenetrable thickets of spruce and fir called Krummholz (known locally and in Newfoundland as tuckamoor). The short growing season, exposure to ice and snow blasting, temperature extremes and poor soils deform and stunt this vegetation, transforming it into patches of bonsai forest. Some of the dwarf spruces in these clumps are so pruned and twisted by wind and ice that they may be 150 years old but have stems only 3 centimetres in diameter. In some areas of hummocky ground, the depressions between adjacent hummocks are completely filled in by a dense snarl of scrubby spruces that rise to about the same general level as the low vegetation which tops the hummocks. From a distance, the surface of such an area appears quite flat and easy to travel, but one soon learns to steer clear of these "tanglefoot" barrens whenever possible. Walking through them is like walking blindly over heaps of broken furniture springs.

The structure of the hummocks themselves, and how they are formed, is interesting. Previous to their formation the ground was covered by a thin mat of mosses and reindeer lichens in which grew various herbaceous plants and shrubs. Where soil conditions are favourable the lichens tend to grow upward, but they are unable to do so to any extent without some sort of support. The needed support is provided by the shrubs. Where they grow close enough together, the shrubs provide a sort of scaffolding upon which the lichens and mosses are able to push upward.

Wind and heavy snowpack often weigh the lowermost branches of both spruce and fir until they acquire a permanent droop and rest on the ground. In a process called layering, roots develop at each point of contact, and a new tree, actually a clone of its parent, develops directly above the new roots. Conifer clones often form very dense circular groups of trees with the original tree at the centre and successively younger trees toward the outside of the circle.

A savannah-like landscape is produced in some areas of the taiga by widely scattered spruce and tamarack trees on an otherwise open plain. The pronounced lean to these trees is a result of the prevailing winds which tends to dry out the side exposed to the wind, but allows a denser growth on the opposite, more protected side.

Caribou herds once roamed these hills, as they did much of eastern Canada. Their numbers declined during the 19th century when their range was drastically reduced by excessive hunting and habitat destruction from forestry, agriculture and fire. In these remote highlands, however, their habitat remained relatively untouched, and some animals persisted here until the 1920s, when they disappeared from overhunting. In 1968 and '69 fifty-one caribou from Quebec were released along this trail in an attempt to reintroduce them to the Park, but the effort proved unsuccessful. The herd was sighted frequently in and near the Park for about a year, but then it declined and finally disappeared around 1974. Nobody really knows why, but it may have had something to do with the white-tailed deer. Deer were absent from Nova Scotia until they were introduced to the western part of the province around 1900. Deer are one of the hosts in the life cycle of a parasitic worm called P. tenuis (*Parelaphostrongylus tenuis* if you want to impress your friends) which gets expelled in their feces. Its larva gets picked up by a snail. The worm usually has no ill effects on deer, but when an infected snail is accidentally ingested by a grazing caribou, it can lead to a lethal neurological disease. The evidence, however, that contact with the white-tail spelled the demise of the transplanted caribou is circumstantial, and the cause of their disappearance will likely never be known.

To get to the trailhead, drive up the Mary Ann Falls road for 5 km and take the road to the left for 0.6 km to the parking lot.

For cross-country skiing, the trail provides ungroomed access to the interior of the Park. There are two ways to get to it: by skiing along the Mary Ann Falls road from the Warren Lake warden station, or from the highway at Black Brook via the network of ski trails (see section on skiing below for details). After the first three kilometres the route is quite exposed, and skiing conditions can be difficult with deep, drifting snow making the trail indistinguishable from the surrounding terrain. The trail is recommended only for experienced skiers with appropriate skills and equipment. About 5 km in from the Mary Ann Falls road there is a small hut that may be rented for overnight camping. It has a wood stove and a couple of wooden bunks but it won't accommodate more than two people unless they get along extremely well.

Broad Cove Beach

The shore north of Warren Brook consists of sand or cobbles, depending on how much is exposed by the tide. This is an easy, seaside walk for about a kilometre along the shore.

The beach at Broad Cove exhibits the interesting pattern of a cuspate beach—a series of shallow troughs and ridges caused by wave action. Beach cusps are thought to be a feature of coasts where wave transport is perpendicular to the shore. The waves come in with their crests more or less parallel to the shore and run up into the pebbly material overlying the packed sand.

The swash reaches beyond the high tide mark and, beginning with tiny depressions, pushes the coarse material aside to form small cusps or ridges which soon join together to make larger ones until they are all about the same size. Without getting bogged down in physics (read: I don't really understand the process!), suffice it to say that the regular pattern they make along the upper part of the beach is related to the frequency and amplitude of the incoming waves.

Above the beach, glacial till overlays crumbling shale, sandstone and limestone cliffs whose layers have been faulted and folded so that in many places they stand on edge. As former mountain ranges of Atlantic Canada wore down, the eroded fragments filled up valleys and low-lying areas on land, or they got carried into rivers, lakes and oceans where they were deposited as sediments. In such basins, they piled up in huge thicknesses—up to 20 kilometres off the Nova Scotian coast. Due to the sheer weight of the deposits combined with the action of minerals that cement the grains together, the sediments became consolidated into rock such as the sandstone and shale in these cliffs.

The limestone here was built up from the limy skeletons of plants and animals that settled on the sea bottom in great thickness, and by chemical means by the precipitation of calcium carbonate from seawater. The rock is full of cavities and solution pockets due to weathering.

The way is blocked at the end of the beach by the steep gneiss and granite cliffs of Little Smokey. In order to get to this part of the shore you have to wade across the outlet of Warren Brook. You may sometimes find the brook too deep to cross, depending upon recent rainfall. If that's the case, another way to get there is by a path leading from the highway 2.4 km north of the campground entrance.

Bear Cove

This stretch of shore is outside the Park, but I think it's worth investigating. Start at the wharf area at the end of The Point road at North Bay Ingonish and follow the shore northward.

The broad limestone ledges with their solution pockets, tide pools and small caverns end in the crumbling, ragged granite cliffs of Red Head, about a kilometre from the wharf. Some scrambling may be required as you get closer to Red Head. Many of the boulders near the wharf were transported there from the surrounding hills by glaciers.

North Bay Beach

The sandy beach at North Bay provides easy walking and is popular for swimming. It is accessible from the day use area about 1/2 km. north of Clyburn Brook.

23. **Franey** ❋ 6 km (3.6 mi) return. Steep.

This trail will burn the carbon out of you. "If you pick 'em up, O Lord, I'll put 'em down" could be your prayer on the steeper parts, but the view is worth it. The 350 m ascent is through mixed woods to a cliff-top lookoff providing breathtaking views of the Clyburn valley and the surrounding highlands, extending ridge upon ridge into the distance. You are in the domain of ravens and eagles here, and they can sometimes be seen below you, soaring among the walls and buttresses of the cliffs. There is a definite change in forest type from Acadian to boreal as you get closer to the summit.

This trail was cut during the summer and fall of 1939 by a group of Forestry Camp workers. The camp was established for young unemployed men, and operated on the site that is now the Ingonish Beach campground. There used to be a fire tower at the summit, but in 1950 it blew down in 160 kilometre per hour winds. It was replaced with a shorter tower, but as its purpose is now served by towers on nearby provincial lands, it was removed by the Park in 1999.

In the mixed woods along the way you may find the acorns of red oaks on the ground. Mice, chipmunks and red squirrels gnaw on these shells to get at the nut inside, leaving an opening in the shell.

Another common tree of the Acadian forest is the beech. It's the one that retains its yellow-brown, papery leaves all winter. The smooth, steel-gray bark of the beech covers the trunk like a tight skin. In the early 1900s, beech was estimated to make up ninety percent of the hardwood forests of Cape Breton, but it no longer thrives here. Many beech trees are afflicted by a fungus that entered North America via Nova Scotia around 1929. The fungus enters openings in the bark created by a sap-sucking insect that is also believed to have found its way to North America via Nova Scotia about 30 years earlier. Cankers caused by the fungus deform the trees, causing them to remain small and spindly. Most large beech trees that have escaped this disease are hollow and provide excellent dens for wildlife.

In springtime, I often find the exquisite fragrance of Nova Scotia's provincial flower, the Mayflower, wafted on the breezes along this trail.

Walking along the trail one day I caught movement among some leaves that littered the path. It was a baby chipmunk, and if it hadn't moved I probably wouldn't have seen it against the dappled ground among the tan leaves and black twigs. As I approached, the little fellow scurried off along the ground and disappeared down a hole near the edge of the path. I'd seen this hole before and wondered if anything ever lived there. Just as I knelt down to look in, the chipmunk poked its head out and, with a startled squeak, dove back down. I moved away a few paces and watched. Soon the little head poked out again, and then another beside it. The two saucy faces looked around, unsure whether or

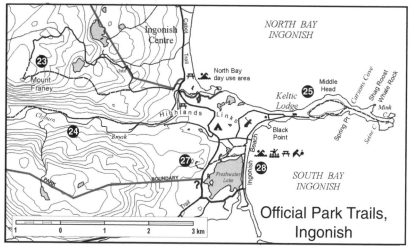

Official Park Trails, Ingonish

not it was safe to come out, but their minds were made up for them when a third sibling, in a hurry to see what was going on, gave them a shove from behind, and they all popped out. As long as I didn't move quickly they didn't seem too disturbed with my presence, and would occasionally scamper very close to my feet.

The neat, round hole must be the entrance to a den. It leads down into the ground for several centimetres and then must veer off horizontally, perhaps to another entrance in the rocks beside the path, because the chipmunks seem to have more than one way of getting in and out. They often make a special work hole which they use when expanding their tunnel systems. It seems they carry excavated dirt in their cheek pouches through the work hole and scatter it someplace on the ground where it doesn't show.

An alternative return route from the top of Mount Franey is the access road that was once used to service the fire tower. The road is a kilometre longer than the path but a little easier on the knees going downhill, and it allows you to make a loop of the hike.

The access road is skiable under the right conditions but inexperienced skiers may find it difficult due to its steepness. It takes about 1/3 time coming down as it does to go up. Spare ski tips—and maybe a cushion to tie on your bum for the descent—would be worth adding to your pack.

The road to the trailhead begins 100 m north of the highway bridge over the Clyburn River.

24. **Clyburn Valley** ❄ 14 km (8.4 mi) return.

The Clyburn Valley is a year-round treat for walkers and cross-country skiers. The level trail along the bottom of the valley provides views of the Clyburn Brook, and the cliffs of Mount Franey. It's a wonderful trail to walk at any time of year, but in autumn, while the leaves are still on the hardwoods, the light that filters through the canopy bathes the woods in a luminescence you can almost feel. When October winds defoliate the trees you can wade ankle-deep through a red, green and golden mosaic of crisp leaves, and the valley becomes redolent with the smells of autumn.

Up until a couple of years ago the first 3 km was maintained as an access road to the trailhead, so it is fairly open and hasn't yet the quiet charm of the rest of the trail. It passes by old fields, alongside views of the Clyburn Brook, and skirts one of the greens of the beautiful Highlands Links golf course.

I witnessed some rather bizarre behaviour on the golf course one day by a couple of hares. They were exceptionally frisky, chasing each other, dashing one way and then another and sometimes coming so close to where I was standing I thought they would collide with me. At one point they appeared to be playing a game of leapfrog, but I later learned that was part of a courtship ritual. Hares will urinate on each other. One of the mating pair will leap into the air and the other will run under the partner and be sprayed with urine. Biologists believe the females can sniff out pheromones from the urine that allows them to gauge a particular male's reproductive efficiency. Chacun à son gout.

About 1.5 km beyond the golf green, and just a few metres past the former trailhead gate, the road comes close to river again. The valley profile shows the classic U shape of glacier-carved valleys, but what is not so apparent is the depth to which glaciers have deepened the valley bottom and subsequently filled it with rock. In periods of low rainfall much of these cobblestones and boulders are exposed, with the river occupying only a small portion of the visible stream bed. At such times it appears that the river is drying up. But there is actually more water in the river here than meets the eye. The bedrock of the channel is another 50 to 100 metres deeper than what can be seen from the trail, so that as much as two thirds of the water that comes down the river actually flows unseen amongst the boulders.

Further along, in the woods beside the trail, are gigantic boulders that have rolled off the mountainside. Not far beyond the boulders are the ruins of a gold mine that operated here between 1912 and 1916. The mine shafts were located in Franey Brook, upstream of the trail, near the base of the mountain. The shafts have long since filled in with erosion but some of the walls and foundations of the buildings remain, and in Franey Brook you can still see parts of an old boiler that was associated with the mine.

As sure as a reel follows a strathspey at a Cape Breton kitchen party, the calls of spring peepers are soon followed by the long-drawn melodious trilling of male toads. You hear them at night in May and June from the shallows of the Park's lakes and streams, or on a moonlight walk along the Trous de Saumons and Clyburn Valley trails. Toads move out from their underground hibernation in the spring. They are mainly terrestrial, going to water only for the mating season. The females lay as many as 12,000 eggs in long, spiral strings of jelly in the water. I've seen the eggs in mud holes or ponds such as Freshwater Lake and Presqu'île Pond. The perfectly spaced little black eggs, enclosed in a rope of transparent invisible jelly, look like doodling in dotted lines all over the mud of the bottom. This rope-like arrangement distinguishes them from the eggs of other frogs and salamanders, which lay their eggs singly or in globular masses. In one or two weeks the coal-black toad tadpoles emerge and through the summer you see them crowding in the warm shallows in such vast numbers that they give the pond margin a sort of black fringe.

They transform into very small toads, tiny enough to fit on your thumbnail, and in late July swarm up onto the land in extremely large numbers. The first time I witnessed this I was dozing one day beside the Aspy River, when I suddenly felt I was in the midst of a plague. Dozens of miniature toads were hurling themselves about on the cobblestones beside the river, and a number of them seemed eager to climb up on my outstretched legs for a better view.

Like other cold-blooded animals toads have no internal means of regulating their body temperature, so if the day is cool they stay in the sunlight and hop around a lot, but if the temperature is hot they rest quietly in a cool shade. You can't get warts from their dry, warty skin, but their skin does have glands that contain a sticky white secretion that is toxic to some animals. If you handle toads, take care not to rub your eyes, as the fluid on your hands will make them sting.

In winter the trail is groomed for skiing for the first 5 km, and there is a warm-up hut at the gold mine ruins. The first 1.5 km of the trail that goes beside parts of the golf course provides an alternate route for skiers.

The trail starts at the parking lot on the north side of the bridge over Clyburn River.

Black Rock

The short, level 200 m (180 yd) trail leads from the road to Middle Head to a lookoff overlooking South Bay.

25. **Middle Head** 4 km (2.4 mi) return with a couple of short, fairly steep sections about 100 m in length.

The smell of spruce and salt air, and the sounds of waves and of seagulls in flight will welcome you as you hike along this sea-bound peninsula. Along the way there are views on both sides of the path of the mountains and sea, and rocky cliffs where you can sit and look for whales or watch the winds and sunlight playing on the surface of the water.

Middle Head was once the estate of a wealthy Ohio industrialist, Henry Corson. After acquiring the property in 1904 he built a large house on it with outbuildings for staff and guests, and ran a farm business there, producing butter and milk that was sold locally. When he died in the 1930s the estate was sold to the government and opened in 1940 as Keltic Lodge.

If you were walking out here almost 300 years ago you would see the sails of dozens of fishing vessels plying the waters surrounding the peninsula, and as you descended to the first rocky cove you would have been greeted by the voices of French fishermen laying out fish on racks to dry. In 1729 the immigration of 180 people from Placentia in Newfoundland led to the establishment of a French settlement and a large chapel at Ingonish. Ingonish became a small thriving port with a population of over 300, providing service to its own land-based fishing fleet as well as to ships from France who called to buy dried cod.

135

Renewal of hostilities between Britain and France led to the demise of the village in 1745, when the British destroyed it to prevent its being used as a base of support during the siege of Louisbourg. Although it continued to be used by French and foreign fishermen for drying fish and mending gear, there was no other permanent settlement here until the early 1800s.

The trail begins as a former wagon road of the Corson estate. After half a kilometre or so the trail starts downhill towards sea level. The path going to the left near the top of the descent takes you to the north side of the peninsula and then in a loop back to the starting point. You could take this as an alternate route on the way back.

Along the trail, carpets of white bunchberry flowers lie among the trees, each quartet of snowy bracts centered in a whorl of green leaves, creating a repeating pattern and symmetry. Further towards the end of the cape, white spruce, one of the few trees able to withstand the salt-laden gales that blow in from the east, is herded into dense clumps at the edge of the fields. Across the bay the lofty mass of Cape Smokey, so named because of the low clouds that often cap its summit, forms a magnificent backdrop. Inland, the broad arc of hills that surround the Ingonish lowlands is cut by steep-sided valleys, creating an irregular skyline along the eastern edge of the highlands. The Clyburn River valley emerges from the interior of the plateau, with the ramparts of Mount Franey challenging hikers to its summit.

Until a few years ago there was a nesting colony of common and Arctic terns on the rocky islet known as Steering Rock at the end of the cape. In 1990 there were 20 to 30 pairs but, every year, they suffered increasing competition from gulls so that their numbers diminished. As park warden Rick Cook puts it, "The gulls took over the best real estate, as they nest a bit earlier than the terns. About the time the terns are sitting on the eggs, the clumsy gulls and their awkward chicks come lumbering through picking up whatever they can scavenge. Terns, being quite territorial, are not real happy about the trespassing gulls." So the terns relinquished their island. As gull numbers decrease with the demise of the fishery and the resulting reduction in waste from fewer fish plants, and the closing of landfill garbage sites, perhaps the terns will one day re-establish their nests on Middle Head.

Somewhere in the woods beside the Middle Head trail there is a boulder on which is chiseled the picture of a sailing ship. I discovered it by accident many years ago. When our children were small my wife and I used to place coins beside the rock and let the children find them there, and they called the rock the "pirate" rock. The illusion of pirates and hidden booty was reinforced one day when a boat with crimson sails sailed around the head and came into the bay. The children spotted the boat just as we were returning from the point and, convinced it was a pirate ship, started to wonder if the pirates would find out who had been meddling with their hidden treasure. I don't know who carved the figure on the rock, or how old it might be. Could it be some 18th-century graffiti, carved by a fisherman from France, or left in more recent times by someone idly passing a summer afternoon on this beautiful peninsula? It's been years since I looked for it and by now it's probably grown over with moss or buried with fallen trees, waiting to be rediscovered.

Another time, as I was following the rugged shore on the north side of the peninsula I came across a beaver clambering down over the rocks towards the water. After traversing the rocks for some distance it slipped into the ocean and began swimming toward the end of the cape. "Odd place for a beaver," I thought, as I groped my way cautiously around a vertical wall of rock, just above the waterline. As I maneuvered around a sharp corner of the rock I suddenly found myself face to face with a bobcat. For a split second I nearly lost my balance, and by the time I recovered enough from the surprise to scramble up the rock to see where it was going, the cat had disappeared. Whether or not it was stalking the beaver I couldn't say, but meeting either one of them out there on the peninsula was entirely unexpected.

You traverse several types of rock on this walk. Granite, the pink rock of the cliffs below Keltic Lodge, forms when magma containing mainly quartz and feldspar solidifies in large masses at considerable depth below the earth's surface. As the old Acadian Mountains eroded away, the underlying crust responded, maintaining equilibrium by floating higher in the plastic layer, just as an ice cube in a glass of water will float higher if you shave off its top surface down to water level. In this way, rocks of Cape Breton Highlands that were formed deep within the earth eventually became exposed at the surface.

During cooling, the original granite mass shrank considerably so that its outer part was broken by systems of fractures. Hot, watery, mineral-laden gases and magma from the core of the intrusion was forced into these openings where they cooled and crystallized, forming thin bands of injected rock called dykes. About half a kilometre along the trail the path descends to an open, grassy saddle with the sea on either side. The rocks on the shore on the north side are cut by bands of red rhyolite and dark basalt. The rhyolite is hardened lava from granitic magma that intruded the crust at shallow depths where, as a result of rapid cooling, large crystals were unable to develop. It is the volcanic, fine-grained equivalent of granite. Granite cools more slowly deeper in the earth, taking up to thousands of years. Basalt, a type of lava, is similar to diorite in mineral content, but contains a larger proportion of darker minerals such as hornblende and olivene.

Boulders along the trail and the cliffs at the end of the headland are diorite. Diorite resembles granite but contains a greater proportion of darker minerals. It's sometimes referred to as salt-and-pepper granite. In places the gray diorite is cut by dykes of pink granite derived from the same magmatic mass that formed Cape Smokey across the bay.

South Bay Beach

The sandy beach is one of the most popular beaches for swimming, sunbathing, or simply walking, in the Park. It's no wonder. You can stroll for over a kilometre along its sandy crescent while admiring the rugged beauty of Middle Head and Cape Smokey. Though we rarely have a chance to view the creatures that live in the sea, we find that the shore itself is home to many kinds of small animals. Twice a day the tides well up and flood the beaches and rocky ledges of the intertidal zone, bringing food and moisture to those that live there. And twice a day the waters recede, allowing us access to this narrow habitat. Ice abrasion and rough waves limit the development of inter-tidal life along much of the Park's coast, and cold water temperatures and a low tidal range reduce the variety of species there.

Still, there are many bits of rock, sand and seaweed along the sea's edge that serve as some happy creature's palace. At low tide, the rock ledges at the north end of the beach are a good place to examine barnacles and periwinkles. Barnacles begin life when they emerge from their parent's shell as a cloud of microscopic, free-swimming larvae. Eventually each settles on its back upon a rock and begins to secrete a cement which will form its protective shell and permanent home. Here, its tissues undergo a complete and drastic reorganization comparable to the metamorphosis of a butterfly larva. From an almost shapeless mass, the rudiments of the shell appear, the head and appendages are moulded, and within twelve hours the complete cone of the shell, with all its plates divided, has been formed.

Step out on the rocks at low tide and all you see is the limy, cone-like shell of six plates. There is no movement, no suggestion of life. But bend down to watch closely after the tide comes in and covers a colony of barnacles. Rhythmically, two tight valves in the centre of each miniature volcano open up, and plume-like feeding appendages wave back and forth acting as a net to pull in microscopic plants and animals from the sea water. The creature inside each shell is something like a small pinkish shrimp that lies head downward, firmly cemented to the base of the chamber that it cannot leave. Only the appendages are ever exposed.

Within its cup of lime, the barnacle faces a dual growth problem. As a crustacean enclosed in a shell, the animal itself must periodically shed its unyielding skin so that its body can enlarge. Difficult as it seems, this feat is successfully accomplished. A container of seawater from the shore may be flecked with the white, semitransparent skins. Seen under the microscope, every detail of structure is perfectly represented. In the cellophane-like casings you can even count the joints of the appendages.

The second problem is that of enlarging the hard cone to accommodate the growing body. Just how this is done no one seems to be sure, but probably there is some chemical secretion to dissolve the inner layers of the shell as new material is added on the outside.

A barnacle that survives the attacks of predators, grinding ice and tumultuous surf may live for as long as three years. After its death the empty shell remains attached to the rock and may serve as a refuge for other forms of life attempting to get a foot-hold on the rocky shore, such as periwinkles. These snails of the intertidal zone do not cling like barnacles, and are easily dis-lodged. They go with the current, surviving storms, as it were, by rolling with the punches. Periwinkles are vegetarian, feeding on seaweeds and on the slippery film of algae that coat the rocks. They use a file-like tongue called a radula, studded with thou-sands of teeth, to rasp the surface as they crawl along. The ra-dula is a continuous belt or ribbon coiled up like a watch spring in the snail's mouth, and as the current teeth become worn down an endless supply of new ones can be rolled up from behind. In a tide pool observed for 16 years by a biologist, periwinkles low-ered the floor by a centimetre as they scraped food from the rocks. Rain, frost and floods, the earth's major forces of erosion, operate on approximately such a scale.

There's opportunity for geologizing, too. From the beach you get a view of several different kinds of rock that make up Middle Head. As you walk toward that end of the beach the shore becomes strewn with rounded pebbles and boulders. You pass under clay banks and exposures of sculpted gypsum. Fur-ther along the bedrock changes to diorite and gabbro, which are exposed in the glaciated knob of Black Head. Further progress along this section of the shore is finally blocked by granite cliffs. Since the minerals in these rocks differ from each other in physi-cal and chemical properties, the rocks that they make up differ in their hardness and resistance to erosion. Gypsum can be scratched with your fingernail, but hard minerals like quartz, a main component of granite, are difficult to scratch even with a knife. But it's not just the hardness of its minerals that makes granite more durable.

Look closely at a piece of coarse granite among the boulders and you can see that its grains—the gray or glassy quartz, the pink feldspar, and the black, platy mica—fit together like a three-dimensional puzzle. This interlocking crystalline structure makes granite a very tough rock. In contrast, the gypsum is built up in layers, with planes of weakness along which it splits easily. That is why the granite headlands of Middle Head and Cape Smokey continue to resist the assaults of the Atlantic, while most of the softer rocks that once lay between them have long since eroded to form the beautiful bay.

In the other direction, towards Smokey, you can follow the barrier beach that extends between Freshwater Lake and the ocean, and to the mouth of Ingonish Harbour. Barrier beaches form when deposits eroded from the surrounding hills and coast are built up into spits by waves and longshore currents. Headlands become linked and barachois (lagoons) or lakes are formed behind them. The bar across Ingonish Harbour is kept open by dredging, but Freshwater Lake, once an inlet of the sea, has become completely cut off.

28. **Freshwater Lake** Wheelchair accessible 1.3-km (0.8 mi) level loop.

This is a pleasant, relaxing walk. The trail follows the shore of Freshwater Lake until it comes to a road that takes you back to the start. Loons breed on this lake every year, and they are commonly heard or seen from the path, sometimes with little ones in tow. What might appear to be an oddly shaped adult can upon closer inspection be a mother loon with her chicks riding on her back. Beavers live in the lake, too, and you can see in places along the trail the stumps of trees that were felled by beavers. The path joins an unused paved road at a tiny inlet of the lake. On the other side of the inlet, a 500 m extension of the path (not accessible by wheelchair) takes you to the start of the Freshwater Lake Lookoff Trail (see below). At the junction of the path and the road is a marsh. See if you can spot the remains of an abandoned beaver lodge there. The marsh is a good place to listen for frogs in the spring and summer.

The first isolated peeps of spring peepers mean that it's time to reluctantly put away my skis for another year, but for winter-weary people they are notes of optimism that spring is finally on the way. These tiny frogs are among the very first to call and breed in the spring, often starting in May while there is still snow on the ground and ice on the lakes. As the nights get warmer you can hear the repetitive peep-peep-peep of their mating calls from just about any pond, marsh or accumulation of water in the woods, fields and roadsides throughout the Park.

The chorus in a pond full of peepers can be almost deafening if you're standing beside it, but the tiny frogs are hard to find. They're only about 3 cm long and they blend in so well with their surroundings that they're difficult to spot. The easiest way to see calling peepers is to look for them on warm nights in May or June with a flashlight and watch for their shiny vocal sacs inflating and deflating as they call. They pump these sacs full of air until they look like a full balloon, then let out a mighty peep while discharging the air. Sometimes peepers make their calls (it's only the males that call) while sitting under clumps of grass or in cracks or crevices in the earth. Such positions act as amplifiers to the call, and also can create an effective ventriloquism, with the sound seeming to come from somewhere other than where the frog actually is.

The trail starts at the South Bay beach (follow the signs from the parking lot).

27. Freshwater Lake Lookoff

This short (150-m/135-yd) trail climbs steeply to a view of Middle Head peninsula, Freshwater Lake and Cape Smokey. The trail starts across the road from the Park administration building, 300 m north of the Ingonish Visitor Centre.

The Old Cabot Trail

After its initial construction during the 1920s and '30s, parts of the Cabot Trail were relocated to less severe or more scenic routes. Within the Park these old abandoned roads are no longer maintained except by the animals that continue to keep a track open along them. It is still possible to find these roads but they are gradually becoming overgrown. I like to follow them because of their historical interest, and for that other age-old excuse— because they're there. They are recommended for experienced hikers only.

One of these sections of the old Cabot Trail begins directly across the highway from the driveway to the Cap Rouge lookoff, 600 m north of Corney Brook campground. From here it follows a winding route up the valley of Canadian Brook for 4 km and emerges at the top of French Mountain across the highway from the driveway to the emergency shelter. Although it's becoming overgrown and requires wending your way in places around alders and saplings, most of it is still fairly easy to follow. It may be hard to find near the upper end, so be prepared to bushwack out to the highway if you happen to lose it (listen for the traffic). At the lower end it starts in the alders about 40 metres from the brook. It's quite steep, and on some turns it clings precariously to the mountainside. It certainly helps one appreciate the amount of labour that went into the building of these roads—and the courage of those who drove on them! This road was in use until the late 1930s, when it was abandoned in favour of the present route of the highway up the valley of Jumping Brook.

The gravel road between the Skyline and Fishing Cove trailheads was also once part of the Cabot Trail. From the Skyline parking lot the road continues 7 km to rejoin the highway at the parking lot for the Fishing Cove trail. An interesting feature of this road is the unusual construction of the wooden bridges that span the ravines at the upper branches of South Fishing Cove Brook. The bridges are not only curved but canted as well, not so much to accommodate fast drivers of the day as to allow water to run off more easily. These bridges are no longer safe and are closed to hikers. In order to cross the brooks you have to scramble down and up the ravines. The present route of the highway, completed around 1960, was chosen to avoid these ravine crossings. About 2.5 km from the northern end of this road is a side road that goes for about a kilometre to an abandoned fire tower. A much earlier road, just a cart track really, wound its way to the hamlet at Fishing Cove following the ridge between South Fishing Cove Brook and the sea, but that old trail has long since disappeared.

The road to Mary Ann Falls was part of the Cabot Trail between North Ingonish and Neil's Harbour until 1949 when the current, more scenic route was built along the coast. The road is gated just beyond the falls, and beyond that it is becoming overgrown. But it continues from the gate for another 4.5 km to rejoin the highway 1.2 km south of Halfway Brook. If you follow this old road for about a kilometre past the gate you come to Black Brook, which is spanned by a one-lane iron bridge.

Another abandoned section of the Cabot Trail remains hidden in the Grande Anse valley. Eight hundred metres east of the MacIntosh Brook campground entrance, part of the old road enters the woods on the south side of the highway, and rejoins the highway about a kilometre further on. A concrete bridge still spans the Grande Anse Brook where the old road crosses it. The old road can be accessed at either end. Its western end is partly hidden behind a mound of earth.

Ski Trails

Many of the Park's hiking trails are often suitable for skiing, depending on snow and weather conditions. They include Warren Lake (groomed to lake), Clyburn Valley (groomed), L'Acadien, Trous de Saumons, Lake Trail, Corney Brook, Skyline, Benjies Lake, Aspy, Glasgow Lakes, Jigging Cove Lake, Branch Pond, and Franey.

Each of these is described in the trails section. For skiing, trail permits are required for all the groomed trails, but skiing is free in other areas of the Park. The permits are available at Park offices and retail outlets in Ingonish. For information on ski trail conditions and which trails are groomed, call (902) 285-2549.

When conditions permit, the trails are groomed five metres wide with a classic track set on the side to permit both skating and classic skiing.

There is also a network of groomed ski trails near Black Brook. These loops are accessible from the highway across from the parking area half a kilometre south of Black Brook bridge. There's a waxing hut with electricity here. The loops vary in length (from 1 to 5.5 km) and in their degree of difficulty. One of these trails connects with the Mary Ann Falls road, which links it to the Branch Pond trail. There are two warm-up huts in the Black Brook ski area that can be reserved and rented for overnight camping. One is located at the trailhead, and the other at Mary Ann Falls. The hut at the trailhead has a concrete floor, electricity, a wood stove and a supply of wood, four tables but no bunks. The hut at Mary Ann Falls has a wood stove, a supply of wood, a table and a long wide bench that doubles as two single bunks. There are pit privies at each site. A small cabin near Branch Pond is also available to rent for ski camping, but it is tiny. Park brochures describe it as basically a wooden tent, just big enough for two people. It has a wood stove, a supply of wood, and two wooden bunks. The phone number to reserve these huts is (902) 285-2691. For information on winter tourist accommodations near the Park, phone Nova Scotia Tourism at 1-800-565-0000.

The Mary Ann Falls road itself is groomed. It's 7 km from the start of the road at Warren Lake warden station to the falls. The road climbs steadily for the first 2.5 km, with minor dips and rises for the rest of the way. At 5 km from the start of the Mary Ann Falls road, the Branch Pond Lookoff trail branches off to the left, and about a kilometre further the trail to the Black Brook loops goes to the right.

Broad Cove Campground provides an easy 3-km groomed loop with a view of the ocean.

6

Off-Trail Exploring

There's pleasure in dragging through peat bogs and bragging
Of all the fine walks that you know;
There's even a measure of some kind of pleasure
In wading through ten feet of snow...

The Manchester Rambler

HIKING OFF-TRAIL in Cape Breton Highlands National Park has its special requirements and challenges, but for those with good navigation skills and a certain degree of fitness, it also has its own rewards. If you plan to stay overnight in the back country you must register with park wardens. Certain areas of the Park contain unique, fragile or endangered features and ecosystems. Preservation is the key consideration here, and in order to give these sensitive areas the greatest possible protection and minimize human impact, overnight camping is not permitted in them. Although long distance backpacking routes for multi-day hikes are not currently well developed in the Park, I've found plenty of places to go and explore on day trips without the inconvenience of having to carry a tent, stove, sleeping bag and all the other specialized gear that's needed on overnight trips. These excursions can be as easy or as difficult as you want to make them.

Off-trail hiking conditions throughout the Park vary considerably with the weather, the steepness and wetness of the terrain, and in the density of the vegetation from one place to another. The walking is easier in woods where the understory is not so thick, and on the more open terrain of bogs and rocky barrens. By trial and error, a map and compass, a little luck and patience, you get to know where the best traveling is. Moose trails often make excellent hiking trails if you can find them going in the direction you want.

Before heading off into the back country consider your ability at route-finding in poor visibility if low clouds settle in. This is a frequent occurrence on the plateau, and all the boundaries and landmarks that could help guide you can be blotted up in grey emptiness, especially on the often-featureless terrain of the barrens.

Distances between places on the topographical map might not appear so great as the crow flies, but it is a different story when the crow is walking and carrying a pack through windfalls and around obstacles. I've sometimes picked out what looked like an interesting spot on the map, only to end up on a sweltering hot day with no breeze and salt sweat running into my eyes, struggling through nearly impenetrable thickets of tuckamoor while being attacked by one of the back country's most ubiquitous carnivores, the deer fly.

I don't mean that traveling in these areas is out of the question; even a misery trip now and then has its redeeming points. But be prepared to find hard going in places, sometimes under crummy conditions.

Other places where I like just wandering around through the woods are some of the broader valley bottoms, like the Grande Anse and Aspy valleys, for example. In springtime and the fall, especially, when there is no greenery on the trees to hide the view, much more of the surrounding hillsides are visible and I find features revealed that I wasn't aware of before: rock faces, small ponds and clearings in the woods, old trails on the sides of hills. In both of these valleys you may come across signs of old homesteads: apple trees, cellars hidden among the spruce, and mossy piles of stone that once marked the edges of clearings. At Grande Anse, before the Park was established there were five farms located south of the highway between MacIntosh Brook campground and the Lone Shieling. The remains of similar habitations can be found in parts of the Aspy valley at Big Intervale, along the upper side of the road to Beulach Ban Falls. The stone fences in the forest speak of the unending toil faced by the pio-neer settlers—toil broken only by the respite of kept Sabbaths, or made less burdensome by a song. Whenever I come upon old cellars like the ones here, I wonder what it must have been like in the middle of February, those long winter nights with the icy blast of the wind in the trees, breaking the ice on a bucket in the morn-ing to draw a dipper of water.

The woman who died one winter's night on the banks of the Aspy River rests in a small graveyard that lies hidden there in the forest. Who else lies there with her, with only fieldstones to mark their final resting place? Someone's child, perhaps, taken with fever? A young man or woman who died of a ruptured appendix before a doctor could reach them? It all reminds me of crop fail-ures and the unfailing generosity of neighbours.

Off-Trail Skiing

By December, the snow starts to accumulate and a whole different world opens up. In the forests of the plateau, fallen logs and undergrowth get buried, uneven surfaces are blanketed with a smooth covering, and travel through the widely spaced trees is easier than it would be in summer without the snow cover. Stream channels become filled in and bridged with snow. On the more open taiga, the snow fills up the hollows between hum-mocks and covers the tuckamoor, and the possibilities for skiing become endless.

There are many places to access the back country directly from the Cabot Trail. Where the highway traverses the tops of French, MacKenzie and North Mountains are good starting points. Since you are already well above sea level at these points, there is really no climbing to do; the slopes are relatively moderate on the rolling plateau. On the eastern side of the Park, Paquette Lake, Mary Ann Falls and Branch Pond Lookoff trails lead into the interior, from where you can branch off on your own. Here the relief is a bit more varied. I often find myself fol-lowing the ridges that form divides between watersheds. Their tantalizing summits give sweeping views across the plateau or down into canyons, and their barren slopes offer exciting downhill runs. Because the plateau slopes seaward on the eastern side, you'll have to do some climbing as you go inland, but that means you get to enjoy a mainly downhill run on the trip out at the end of the day.

As spring approaches, the days grow longer and you don't have to turn back so soon. The weather is a little more temperate than in January or February, and the snow is firmer underfoot. You can linger to watch the scenery, basking in the strengthening rays of the sun. Sometimes I'll come across my ski tracks from a few days before standing in relief, forming parallel rails where the uncompacted snow around them melted or blew away. Beside them may be a string of small pedestals, the elevated footprints of a curious coyote that followed my tracks for a while.

There were warm days in April when I headed inland and it seemed that the snow was shrinking by the hour. I'd follow leads between ridges across the barrens, skiing across the springy tuckamoor between patches of melting corn snow, trying to link up one patch of snow with another.

Snow bridges sometimes collapsed behind me as I barely made it across streams, wondering how I was going to get across on my return. (Now I carry a couple of heavy-duty garbage bags for wading streams when I can't find a snow bridge or a log. Pulled on over my boots, they're usually good for one or two crossings before they begin to leak too badly.) By the end of April, snow in the lowlands has largely disappeared, but I often find good skiing, especially on the Park's eastern slopes, until mid-May.

Don't forget to tell someone you're going and what time to expect to hear from you. Better still, leave them with a map of your intended route, or leave one on your windshield or dashboard. Skiing conditions can be difficult when the snow surface becomes compacted into crust by wind, or icy due to rain. Sometimes in the spring the snow can be soft under a sunny sky, but freeze to a crust by late afternoon as the temperature drops. Navigating becomes tricky when low clouds reduce visibility in featureless terrain, and in storms that bring bitter winds laden with stinging snow or lashing rain. Those aren't the only hazards in the back country. One day I was zipping downhill on a wooded slope when a moose suddenly stood up in front of me. I shouted, and if he hadn't voluntarily moved to one side of my line of travel I would have creamed him. Not that I would have done him any damage if I hit him, but I probably would have broken the tips of my skis. Or my neck. I fell when I hit the hollow in the snow where the moose had lain. It looked like a shallow grave. As I floundered around in the snow trying to get up, the moose stood by a few metres away, watching me curiously with a "You do this often?" look on his face.

Often in the heat of summer I've cast a longing glance across the rolling green hills, picturing them covered in snow and recalling some of the winter trips I made there in the past. My mind goes back to a frosty morning in February and I remember heaving my pack up on top of the snowbank at the edge of the highway and climbing up after it, looking forward to four days of solitary skiing.

Swirling gray clouds and flurries obliterate the distant hills. As I hoist the pack onto my back I wonder if the old wooden skis have developed any cracks that I don't know about. Standing there clamped onto the skis, strapped into the pack, and gripping the poles for balance I feel as if I'm at the controls of a kind of traveling contrivance. At the controls, perhaps, but not necessarily in control. Looking up the grade ahead of me I take a tentative step, planting one ski, testing the grip. It holds and I don't sink. Great! A firm base with a few inches of powder on top.

After a few minutes I get to the top of the hill. The clouds begin to dissipate and the sky gets brighter. Patches of blue sky appear through rents in the parting clouds. Striding along the level now, I settle into a relaxed rhythm. The sun comes out again, turning the landscape from gray to white, the sky from gray to deep blue. It's turning into a beautiful day.

And what a view! On the right the hills fall away toward the Sunrise Valley, with the consecutive ridges of the Aspy hills forming a striking backdrop all the way to Money Point. The range is capped in low clouds to about 100 metres below their summit. At the top of the hill before Paquette Lake I give a couple of hard pushes and let gravity take me down toward the lake, watching the scenery go by me as I ski. Just standing there on the skis, coasting smoothly along, feeling the gentle breeze cooling me off, a muffled *sssssss* comes from under the skis as they slip along. It's so relaxing I think I could almost fall asleep. Fantastic!

After Paquette Lake the trail starts uphill again and I begin to see those open barren stretches ahead, all white and glittering. Soon I leave the woods behind and am out on the sunny barrens, moving along at a leisurely pace, trying to see in every direction at once. The branches of the trees are totally hidden by mounds of sparkling white snow. Clumps of trees are so plastered with snow that they look like herds of giant snowmen. What animals might be watching me go by from the hollows underneath their branches? I poke at one of these rounded pillows with a ski pole to see if I can knock it down, but it's so firm that I can only sway the branches slightly. Our kids would crawl inside these cavities like rabbits, and try to scare us when we skied by.

After a while the trail emerges on a wide expanse of rolling barrens. A little later I realize I'm no longer on the trail. Everything is so open here, so windswept, that it's hard to see any sign of it under the snow. The surface is icy from the wind, and tricky to ski on. I try walking without the skis. The crust holds my weight for a few steps, then I break through it, tripping against the edge of the crust. A couple of more steps and I fall through again. This is too hard on the shins! I put the skis on again and aim them down the slope to where I think the trail is. Skittering and clattering across the polished surface on a wing and a prayer, I complete half a revolution, continue skiing backwards for several metres, and end up conducting a tree resiliency test at the bottom of the slope.

Before long I'm working my way up a steep part of the trail. It's steep enough that I have to herringbone and soon I'm sweating from the exertion. In places the branches are bowed over the path with their burden of snow. I punch at the clumps of snow with my ski pole, trying to knock them off so that the weighted limbs will spring back up, for there will be no stopping on the way out on this hill once I start down it unless I snag one of those branches!

There are over two metres of snow on the level up here. Except for the opening cut through the trees, there would be no way to distinguish the trail. Soon, however, the woods give way to barrens again. There's no more sign of a trail now, just the snowy barrens stretching mile after mile into the distance. I head over towards a lake hoping to find open water where the brook enters it at its far end. Boy, is this area exposed! It has gotten cloudy again and the wind is picking up. The clouds reduce the visibility and everything is starting to look gray. I ski back and forth around the west end of the lake, looking for the brook, but I can't find it, and I can't remember where the path is. How quickly the weather changes up here. How easily your frame of mind changes, too! I've soon got to get out of here and find some wooded shelter.

I get out the map to check my bearings. When all else fails, read the instructions. The wind nearly tears it from my hands and when I grab for it I drop a mitten and have to go chasing after it, nearly dropping the map again. It doesn't take long to figure out where I am. Whoops, wrong lake. I should have been paying closer attention. According to the map I have to ski to the south to hit the lake I'm looking for. I could head directly across the one I'm at, but the wind has swept the snow off of it down to the bare ice, and I begin to wonder what it would be like trying to pitch the tent in this wind with a broken wrist. No, better retrace my route around the end of the lake, then head south to pick up the brook that comes out of the other lake. That should be no problem. Unless it turns into a real whiteout before I get there. And doesn't let up for a couple of days. I should have taken a bearing on that last hill back there where I lost the trail. Even now I'm not sure which side of it I have to go on to find the trail back out. Forget about that for now, though. SKI OR DIE. That's what the logo says that's stuck on the top of one of my skis. My teen-aged son designed it for me one year in Computer class. The wind is getting fierce now, driving ice pellets before it, and it's dark. Just keep following the compass. The brook should be up ahead.

I keep on across the barrens and without realizing it, ski across the brook. It's completely filled in with snow. I find a good site for the tent, surrounded on the windward side by a clump of fir trees and on two other sides by snowdrifts. It looks quite snug, actually, sheltered from the wind. So it's off with the skis and pack, then stamp out an area big enough for the tent. Not too close to the trees, though. If some of those big chunks of frozen snow came down in the wind...! I wonder how sound that tree trunk is. Any chance that the crown is going to break off and topple onto the tent? Probably not, unless the winds get any worse. I hope.

After the tent is pitched, the next job is to stamp out a place around the entrance for cooking. Get the stove out, pour the last of my water into a pot and find a granola bar to tide me over until supper's cooked. Meanwhile, roll out the sleeping bag inside the tent. Remove anorak, shirt and pants; quickly pull on long johns and down jacket; then replace pants, shirt and anorak. How's the water coming? Ah, a few bubbles starting to form on the bottom of the pot. I'm starving. The covered pot burps, releasing a little cloud of steam that signals the water is boiling. Some of the water gets poured into a pot of beef stroganoff, the remainder is put back on the burner and more snow is added to make up enough water to replenish the canteen. Maybe tomorrow I can find a hole in the brook, to save me from having to melt snow.

After the main course I find a couple of squished pastries in the pack, and wash them down with a cup of hot chocolate. It's starting to snow again. But in spite of the wind and the darkness a warm feeling of security and satisfaction permeates my little space, a feeling enhanced by a full stomach.

Time to get into the sleeping bag now. The nylon is cool at first, but with a little squirming and wriggling as I put on a pair of dry socks, there is enough heat generated to turn it into a cozy cocoon. At six o'clock I settle down to read by the light of a candle lantern. My legs ache mildly, and I relish the sensation of limbs becoming heavy and relaxed as muscles give in to fatigue. The wind is howling through the trees, but the walls of the tent move only slightly in the shelter of the drift. At half-past eight I can fight sleep no longer. I blow out the candle, snuggle down into the sleeping bag and settle in for a long winter nap.

6.30 a.m. It doesn't sound good. I poke my head out the door. Through thick clouds and blowing snow I faintly make out the silhouettes of some nearby trees. So much for the forecast of partly cloudy. I'd like to phone the weather office and tell them that so far nearly a foot of partly cloudy has fallen since their forecast. Through the night it developed into a storm with high winds and I had to dig the tent out to relieve the weight of snow on the sides. After a bowl of porridge I go back inside the tent and wait.

The morning passes, and with the weather showing no sign of letting up, it doesn't look like I'll be able to travel as far as I originally planned. Maybe I should stay here and take day trips instead of packing up and moving on. In that case I could build myself a snow hut. The wind is after coming around from a different direction and the trees no longer protect the tent. And it will give me something to do. Using an aluminum shovel, it takes about three hours to make the snow house—an hour to pile up a mound of snow, half an hour to let the snow settle and consolidate, and an hour or so to hollow it out. Now I don't have to worry about dragging snow inside every time I come or go, or spilling things on the floor. And I won't have to listen to the incessant flapping of the tent walls.

Two o'clock, still blowing. What a wild place this is! Sweeping down across the open moor the wind blows up clouds of powder, reducing visibility to a hundred metres at times. I stay in the snow hut reading Alan Moorhead's history of the early exploration of Central Africa and the search for the source of the Nile River. The book recounts the experiences of men like David Livingstone, and their stories of hardship and perseverance against disease, mosquitoes, tropical swamps and the equatorial climate. Great stuff! It seems to add a little warmth to the hut and to make the boredom of confinement a little more tolerable.

In the afternoon the drifting abates a little so I go out to stretch my legs and roam around a bit. I put on my skis and tack for a kilometre or so into the wind to the brow of a low hill, then sail along its crest before dropping down its side to lower ground. Here and there are scattered tamaracks and stunted spruce with the perennial lean to them that comes with being exposed to these winds. Now and then a squall hides from view any distinguishing features of the landscape, so I can't stray very far from the shelter. I ski beside long drifts that are remarkably sculpted by the wind, and try to figure whether the graceful shapes have been carved out of a snowbank or have drifted into these forms to begin with. I stand and watch continuous streams of frozen particles swishing across the packed surface, driven by the constant winds, intertwining, shifting, blending and forming cross-bedded layers and elegant cornices, till a gust sends me slithering and I sail across to examine another drift.

I ski over into the hollow where the brook is, but here the snow is powdery and deep and I wind up trying to extricate a pole from among the branches of the buried tuckamoor as I pole over it.

That night it snows again and continues to drift. I awake around 5 a.m. to find the moon out in a clear, starry sky, then go back to sleep and get up a little before dawn. Gradually the mood of the snowy landscape changes from a frosty, pre-dawn ghostliness, through different hues of rose and amber as the sun rises. The first direct rays shine yellow through a haze of airborne crystals that are drifting in the wind. Finally there is dazzling whiteness under a blue sky, without a cloud in sight.

The wind dies down, and after a steaming breakfast of porridge I set off for the day. Everywhere the trees are caked with snow, white monuments in a glittering white landscape. The woods look like a Christmas card scene. In places you can't even see through the branches. I follow a brook, sometimes skiing along the unobstructed corridor between the woods on either side of the stream, which flows silently underneath the snow, sometimes through the woods themselves, among its openings and passageways, until I come to a lake. There are so many places to go here it's hard to decide which direction to take.

I ski along the edge of the lake for a while, mindful of any places where brooks might be running into it and creating open water. I often used to take shortcuts across lakes, sometimes using the presence of moose tracks as confirmation that the ice was safe enough to ski on, until one day I saw tracks leading to an opening in the middle of a lake. There was only one set of tracks leading to the open water. I've been cautious about crossing lakes ever since.

I strike out over the barrens, climbing gentle slopes to the tops of low rises and knolls, then slip back down their slopes to head up others. From the higher ground I can see in all directions across the terrain. To the west the snow-covered barrens stretch to the horizon, providing good skiing for miles. Some areas are not entirely treeless but it's easy working your way through the thinly wooded areas. Later in the day I find myself on a ridge with the deep valley of Black Brook dropping away beside me as I ski along its crest.

In the afternoon I turn around and start following my tracks back toward camp. Helped along by a light breeze at my back, I make the return trip in less time than I expected. It's four o'clock but I feel like I can go on for hours. There is still an hour or so of daylight left so I roam around the hills in the vicinity of the camp, then head over to the brook. It is easy following the brook downstream; gliding down the shallow gully without even poling is like drifting along with the current in a canoe, with the banks slipping by. As I round a curve I nearly ski into a moose.

The next day dawns with a hazy sky and a halo around the weak sun foretelling another storm on the way. But my trip is coming to an end. After packing up, I spend a couple of hours touring some ridges and hollows before coming back to the camp to pick up my pack. The trip out will be mostly downhill so I can afford to take some detours along the way. I make my way up onto a windy knoll for a last look. Facing west I can see my tracks from the day before disappearing over a knoll, then rising up over another ridge and finally disappearing in the distance. Turning toward the east I see the trail out leading away from the barrens and into the woods. I sidestep over to the edge of the hill, point the skis out over the crest, and let the wind push me off onto the fall line.

End Note

"USE AND ENJOYMENT have been among the historical goals for Canada's national parks, and must continue to be major elements of the Canadian character and heritage. In order to protect ecological integrity, human use in national parks must be based on the principle of responsible experience: use without abuse. Human use must also pass the dual tests of allowability and appropriateness." (One of the key findings of the Panel on Ecological Integrity, a group of scientists concerned with ensuring the long term health of Canada's national parks.)

Over the years there have been major changes in the landscape of Nova Scotia due to industrial, commercial and recreational development. Degradation due to the ease of motorized access is increasing, and in nearly all of Nova Scotia outside of its national parks it is almost impossible to find yourself more than three or four kilometres from a road that is passable by motor vehicle. All-terrain and over-snow vehicles have greatly extended the range of machines capable of further despoiling the remaining wilderness. Each new edition of the topographic maps records changes in land use in and around Cape Breton Highlands National Park, showing how rapidly these changes come about and how vulnerable the Park itself is to the cumulative effects of various influences that originate both inside and outside its boundaries. In the 1950s a large section of the watershed of the beautiful Faribault Brook, a tributary of the Chéticamp River, was deleted from the Park to accommodate mining interests. In the 1970s a section of the Park surrounding Chéticamp Lake was turned over to the provincial government for hydroelectric development. Much of the Park's southern boundary is visible as a wall of trees that rise adjacent to massive forest clearcuts.

When Cape Breton Highlands National Park was established in 1936, its primary purpose was to stimulate economic development through tourism, and early Park development focused on completion and improvement of the Cabot Trail and the construction of recreational facilities. The construction of roads and highways, trails, campgrounds, recreational and administration facilities, and the wear and tear by half a million visitors a year have led to many adverse impacts on the Park. Its ecosystems have been diminished by such things as loss of habitat; disturbances to wildlife; deposition of airborne pollutants; introduction of exotic plants and animals; and disappearance of native species. The same kinds of changes threaten many of Canada's national parks, with the result that management objectives for Parks have since shifted, placing primary emphasis on the protection of their ecological integrity rather than their use as just playgrounds. The threats and impacts are not always obvious to the casual or first-time visitor, and so it sometimes seems that the rules that limit where we go and what we do in our national parks are too stringent and somewhat arbitrary, until we understand how much effect our combined activities have had.

We can not assume that our national parks will continue to exist unimpaired just because they are protected—that they will survive independently of the state of their surrounding landscape. As the wild lands of Cape Breton are diminished and the boundary between Park and "not Park" becomes more pronounced, it becomes evident that the survival of Cape Breton Highlands National Park is closely tied to the attitudes, beliefs and ways of life of people who use the Park and its surroundings. This natural heritage is only as safe as people, knowing about it, want it to be.

APPENDIX A
Vital Information

Cape Breton Highlands National Park
Ingonish Beach, Nova Scotia, Canada B0C 1L0
www.parkscanada.gc.ca
atlantic.parksinfo@pc.gc.ca
Ingonish Beach Phone (902) 285-2691
Ingonish Beach Fax (902) 285-2866
Chéticamp Phone (902) 224-2306/3403
Chéticamp Fax (902) 224-2445

Warden Offices
Ingonish Beach (902) 285-2542/2543
Chéticamp (902) 224-3798

Highlands Links Golf Course
Tom.Forsythe@pc.gc.ca
highlands.links@pc.gc.ca
1-800-441-1118
(902) 285-2624/2600
Fax (902) 285-2111

Campgrounds
Ingonish, Broad Cove, Big Intervale
MacIntosh Brook, Corney Brook, Chéticamp

Picnic Sites
Ingonish, Warren Lake, Mary Ann Falls, Black Brook
Neil's Brook, MacIntosh Brook, Grande Anse, Trout Brook, La Bloc
La Grande Falaise, Chéticamp Visitor Centre

Supervised Beaches
Ingonish Beach and Freshwater Lake

Unsupervised Beaches
Petit Étang (salt and fresh water), Presqu'île, Corney Brook
Black Brook (salt and fresh water), Broad Cove
Warren Lake (fresh water), and North Bay Ingonish

Emergency Shelters
North Mountain, MacKenzie Mountain, French Mountain
These huts are provided for motorists who have broken down or are
otherwise in need of emergency assistance. They are equipped with
wood stoves and firewood; the huts on MacKenzie and French Mountains have telephones, with a list of local emergency phone numbers.

Radio Stations, English
CBC-AM (Canadian Broadcasting Corporation)
Sydney at 1140, Charlottetown at 1070
CBC-FM Sydney at 90.1, 93.9, 94.3, 107.1
CJCB-AM at 1270 and CHER-AM at 950, Sydney
CJFX-AM at 580, Antigonish
CHTN-AM at 720, Charlottetown
CKPE-K94 (FM) Sydney
CJFX-FM at 98.9, Antigonish

Radio Stations, French
SRC-FM (Société Radio-Canada) at 107.5
CKJM-FM at 106.1, Chéticamp

Other Phone Numbers
EMERGENCY: 911
Weather Information Cape Breton Island (902) 564-7357
Travelers Weather 1-900-565-5555 (user fee applies)
Tourism Cape Breton (902) 539-9876
Summer Festivals and Events 1-888-562-9848
Nova Scotia Tourist Information 1-800-565-0000

APPENDIX B
Whales in Cape Breton's Waters

THE UNEXPECTED GLIMPSE of a wild animal is always an exciting prospect, whether it's of the big fierce variety or not. But when you're standing at a lookoff (or sitting in a kayak) and suddenly realize there's a whole herd of large mammals ploughing through the ocean in front of you, it's a privilege indeed. I've often seen this spectacle from several of the higher lookoffs along the Cabot Trail, such as those on Little Smokey, MacKenzie Mountain and French Mountain. From early May to late November whales and dolphins migrate to the waters surrounding the Park. Some species are more commonly seen than others. Minke and fin whales are often seen from whale cruises, but the most commonly sighted from the Cabot Trail is the long-finned pilot whale. This medium-size whale, also known as the pothead because of its high, rounded forehead, reaches just over 6 metres in length, and large males may weigh close to 3 tonnes (3300 pounds). Pilot whales are very gregarious. They often travel in herds of several hundred, closely coordinating their activities and movements. They live throughout the year in deep water, and are especially abundant on the continental slope. They appear in the shallow waters of the Atlantic coast and in the Gulf of St. Lawrence during summer with the arrival there of dense swarms of migrating squid and mackerel, their principal prey.

Although sightings are not common, several other species migrate to the waters surrounding the Park to take advantage of the nutrient-rich waters. It's thought that all the blue whales of the North Atlantic summer in the Gulf of St. Lawrence. Over 30 metres long, the blue whale is the largest animal ever known on

Earth. Sei, humpback and sperm whales have been reported off-shore. A young beluga whale lingered in the waters of South Bay Ingonish for several weeks one summer, much to the delight of swimmers at Ingonish Beach. Orcas can occasionally be spotted from more northerly points on the island. From the lookoffs on MacKenzie Mountain I've seen groups of white-sided dolphins leaping, spinning and lobtailing clear out of the water as they travel rapidly along.

The Whale Interpretive Centre at Pleasant Bay provides information about whales and how to identify them, as well as opportunities for whale watching—and a full-size replica of a pilot whale.

THERE ARE SEVERAL WAYS to distinguish between different kinds of whales when you are relatively close to them, but from a distance it's not quite as easy. The following illustrations and remarks might be useful in identifying these majestic animals from shore:

Pilot whale

Blow is low and barely visible at a distance
Bulbous blunt head; dorsal fin is thick with long base
Most common whale in Park waters; seen in groups from 5 to 200

Minke whale

Blow is low and barely visible at a distance
Top of head and dorsal fin usually surface at same time; narrow pointed
    snout sometimes breaks the surface
Dorsal fin extremely pointed and slightly hooked backward
Commonly seen close to shore, usually singly, sometimes in pairs

Fin whale

Blow tall and column-shaped or cone-shaped
Head appears first, immediately blows, then long back appears,
    then dorsal fin
Dorsal fin curved and rather pointed
Head wedge-shaped; right lower jaw white, left lower jaw dark
Usually seen in small groups of 2 to 8, sometimes singly

Appendix B: Whales in Cape Breton Waters

Sei whale

Blow column-shaped or cone-shaped
Head, blow and dorsal fin often visible at nearly the same time,
        just after blow
Head flat and wedge-shaped
Usually seen singly or in groups of 2 to 10

**Humpback
whale**

Blow bushy, balloon-shaped—often seen first—then the back
Dorsal fin variable in shape
Long white flippers 1/3 of body length
Wart-like bumps on head
Flukes lifted out of water on terminal dive
Seen singly or in small groups of 2 to 8; inshore sightings are infrequent

Blue whale

Blow column-shaped or cone-shaped
Dorsal fin far back & very small, often only visible just before animal is
        about to dive
Flukes lifted out of water on terminal dive
Most positive trait is the large size
Sightings are uncommon

Sperm whale

Blow directed forward & to the left; blowhole is well forward on head
Head and blow are seen first, then the back
Head is blunt and square
Low dorsal fin and a series of lumps along the back
Flukes lifted out of water on terminal dive
Inshore sightings are uncommon

Orca

Tall pointed dorsal fin
Inshore sightings are uncommon